The Library Staff Development Handbook

MEDICAL LIBRARY ASSOCIATION BOOKS

The Medical Library Association (MLA) features books that showcase the expertise of health sciences librarians for other librarians and professionals.

MLA Books are excellent resources for librarians in hospitals, medical research practice, and other settings. These volumes will provide health care professionals and patients with accurate information that can improve outcomes and save lives.

Each book in the series has been overseen editorially since conception by the Medical Library Association Books Panel, composed of MLA members with expertise spanning the breadth of health sciences librarianship.

Medical Library Association Books Panel

About the Medical Library Association

Founded in 1898, MLA is a 501(c)(3) nonprofit, educational organization of 3,500 individual and institutional members in the health sciences information field that provides lifelong educational opportunities, supports a knowledge base of health information research, and works with a global network of partners to promote the importance of quality information for improved health to the health care community and the public.

Books in the Series:

The Medical Library Association Guide to Providing Consumer and Patient Health Information edited by Michele Spatz
Health Sciences Librarianship edited by M. Sandra Wood
Curriculum-Based Library Instruction: From Cultivating Faculty Relationships to Assessment edited by Amy Blevins and Megan Inman

Mobile Technologies for Every Library by Ann Whitney Gleason

Marketing for Special and Academic Libraries: A Planning and Best Practices 6. Sourcebook by Patricia Higginbottom and Valerie Gordon

Translating Expertise: The Librarian's Role in Translational Research edited by Marisa L. Conte

Expert Searching in the Google Age by Terry Ann Jankowski

Digital Rights Management: The Librarian's Guide Edited by Catherine A. Lemmer and Carla P. Wale

The Medical Library Association Guide to Data Management for Librarians Edited by Lisa Federer

Developing Librarian Competencies for the Digital Age Edited by Jeffrey Coghill and Roger Russell

New Methods of Teaching and Learning in Libraries by Ann Whitney Gleason

Becoming a Powerhouse Librarian: How to Get Things Done Right the First Time by Jamie Gray

Assembling the Pieces of a Systematic Review: A Guide for Librarians Edited by Margaret J. Foster and Sarah T. Jewell

Information and Innovation: A Natural Combination for Health Sciences Libraries Edited by Jean P. Shipman and Barbara A. Ulmer

The Library Staff Development Handbook: How to Maximize Your Library's Most Important Resource by Mary Grace Flaherty

The Library Staff Development Handbook

How to Maximize Your Library's Most Important Resource

Mary Grace Flaherty

ROWMAN & LITTLEFIELD
Lanham • Boulder • New York • London

Published by Rowman & Littlefield
A wholly owned subsidiary of The Rowman & Littlefield Publishing Group, Inc.
4501 Forbes Boulevard, Suite 200, Lanham, Maryland 20706
www.rowman.com

Unit A, Whitacre Mews, 26-34 Stannary Street, London SE11 4AB

British Library Cataloguing in Publication Information Available

Library of Congress Cataloging-in-Publication Data Available

ISBN 978-1-4422-7035-0 (hardback : alk. paper) | ISBN 978-1-4422-7036-7 (pbk. : alk.
paper) | ISBN 978-1-4422-7037-4 (electronic)

♾™ The paper used in this publication meets the minimum requirements of
American National Standard for Information Sciences—Permanence of Paper
for Printed Library Materials, ANSI/NISO Z39.48-1992.

Printed in the United States of America

Contents

List of Figures and Tables   ix

Preface   xi

Acknowledgments   xiii

1   Essential Background   1

2   Staffing and Organizational Planning   9

3   Attracting the Best and Brightest   29

4   Staff Engagement: Creating Opportunities   45

5   Staff Development   73

6   Staff Evaluation   93

7   Additional Funding Sources for Staffing Activities   115

8   Going Forward   125

Index   137

About the Author   139

List of Figures and Tables

Figures

Figure 1.1	Traits of Leaders	3
Figure 4.1	Motivation Continuum	47
Figure 4.2	Steps of the Progressive Discipline Process	57
Figure 5.1	Wordle of SILS Survey Results	78
Figure 5.2	Opportunities for Staff Involvement	83
Figure 5.3	Cycle of Staff Development	86
Figure 6.1	Cycle of Goal Setting, Feedback, and Performance	97
Figure 6.2	Components of the Feedback Process	108

Tables

Table 2.1	Select Keys for Strategic Planning Success	15
Table 3.1	Rubric for Evaluating Interviewees' Responses	39
Table 3.2	Example of a Rubric for Evaluation of Candidates' Problem-Solving Skills	40
Table 6.1	Using Goals and Objectives to Guide Expectations and Tasks	97

Preface

An exceptional library of any type requires exceptional staff, individuals who are enthusiastic, engaged, and willing to go the extra mile. Identifying, recruiting, and developing exceptional staff are not automatic processes, however, and practitioners often list staff development as a skill they have had to acquire on the job. *The Library Staff Development Handbook: How to Maximize Your Library's Most Important Resource* serves as a guide for aspiring librarians and library managers and any individuals who are responsible for hiring and supervising staff in all types of library settings. It provides a template for systematic operationalization of critical staff-related tasks and activities to optimize library function across institutional settings.

Each chapter in this volume is dedicated to a different aspect of staff interaction and development with practical examples, samples, tips, and anecdotes from a variety of library practitioners and settings. We begin with chapter 1, an introduction to the topic of library staff development. Chapter 2 covers staffing within the context of the greater organization, including strategic planning for developing the workforce and responding to the user community. Job descriptions, succession planning, and cross-training are also covered in chapter 2. Recruitment is discussed in chapter 3, with attention to the interview process, how to design a rubric for evaluating candidates, and how to ensure your job offer is irresistible. Chapter 4 continues with staff engagement and retention, including how to keep staff motivated by recognizing extrinsic and intrinsic factors, and how to challenge staff in a way that they are not overwhelmed. The more demanding side of supervision is also addressed, with a discussion of progressive discipline that includes examples of how to navigate the process.

Chapter 5 focuses on staff development specifically with regard to training and continuing education, activities for mentoring, and maintaining high morale. The next chapter is dedicated to staff evaluation. The process for instituting a regular schedule of performance appraisals is introduced, along with suggestions for involving staff in the process and how to use goals and objectives as an effective means for assessment. Chapter 7 looks at alternative funding sources for supporting staff, including grants, scholarships, and awards. The final chapter concludes with a summation on staff development and future considerations.

Library staff are indeed the most important resource in every type of library, and tending to staff development is a vital component of an effective manager's repertoire of skills. This volume can serve as a refresher for seasoned directors, as a handbook for new supervisors, as a reference for individuals with supervisory responsibilities, and as a companion text for library management instructors.

Author's note: Throughout this book I have used the pronoun they *and corresponding* their *and* them *to connote* s/he *and* her/his *and* her/him. *This was not an oversight, but rather a deliberate choice, made in an attempt to be inclusive to readers who self-identify in a variety of manners.*

Acknowledgments

I would like to express my sincere gratitude to the following people whose support has made writing this book an enjoyable experience: Charles Harmon, Sami Kaplan, and Les Roberts. Sincere thanks also to contributors Yael Chartier, Lori Haight, Samantha Kaplan, S. Rebecca Lubin, Annie Norman, Curtis Powell, Joan Petit, Alena Principato, David Seleb, and Rebecca Vargha for their valuable input.

This volume is dedicated to my mother, Margaret Jane Flaherty, who gave me my first lessons in "staff development."

Chapter One

Essential Background

"If your actions inspire others to dream more, learn more, do more, and become more, you are a leader."

—John Quincy Adams

"The most powerful leadership tool you have is your own personal example."

—John Wooden

The organizational mission in any type of library setting likely includes some type of service provision, whether it is patent searches in a special library, teen programs in a public library, or access to research databases in an academic library setting. Therefore, if we consider libraries from the perspective of their organizational purpose, at their core they are *service* organizations. Use of the services and resources that are offered is generally voluntary, though; in most settings, it is the users' choice whether to patronize the organization or not. A key factor in that choice is likely the experiences patrons have when they interact with library resources and staff. This chapter introduces considerations for providing an organizational atmosphere that is supportive and nurturing for staff, including leading by example, providing predictable procedures, and responding to challenges.

LIBRARY STAFF

In most library settings, staff are the primary interface with the user community. They are often the first point of contact for patrons, and so they become

1

the face of the organization. Together, library staff interact with the facilities' resources to make the important work happen. In the best circumstances, they inject vitality, project enthusiasm, and keep the organization humming along steadily. In less fortunate cases, they may impede or even obstruct positive relationships with the user community.

In successful organizations, staff development is a continuous, integral, and ongoing process. It encompasses appreciation and support for staff; encouragement, provision of, and allowance for training; continuing education; and professional development opportunities. Staff development also allows for creation of space for individual personalities to interweave with the institutional and organizational culture.

An effective supervisor is always on the lookout for ways to encourage staff to take advantage of new opportunities to keep their skills current, to expand their horizons, and to learn new things. Regular and objective feedback is another component of staff support, and can be as informal as recognition for positive steps toward completion of a project or expressing appreciation for innovative ideas. More formal feedback, such as goals- and objectives-based performance appraisals (as discussed in chapter 6), is another mechanism for communicating to staff they are valued and their contributions are important, while ensuring the organizational mission is being pursued.

There are at least three areas that directly affect individual staff members' fulfillment in the workplace. These include interaction and relationship with their supervisors; institutional rules, structures, and assets; and the employees themselves. Thus, a logical first step in examining staff development is to consider the skills and traits that characterize effective and inspirational supervisors.

LEADING BY EXAMPLE

There is an old quote that demonstrates the challenge of working with an array of individuals with different propensities and personalities: "The optimist proclaims that we live in the best of all possible worlds; and the pessimist fears this is true" (Cabell 1926). Most everyone can describe an individual who has been inspirational and has had a positive effect on them. In an ideal employment scenario with fortunate circumstances, this person might be one's boss, but the inspirational person might also be a coach, teacher, colleague, sibling, friend, and so on. At the same time, most everyone has had experience with individuals who have the opposite effect, and who seem to instill negativity wherever they go. This is a simplistic manner of categorization, but the point I wish to make is that we can learn from both types of individuals and influences.

Figure 1.1. Traits of Leaders

Leaders are those individuals who turn "problems" into opportunities; they are able to maintain a sense of optimism, even in dire circumstances, in order to inspire their colleagues to do the same. Few people are born leaders, though, so what are some of the qualities that can be cultivated to become a leader, to be that person who inspires others? Figure 1.1 depicts some of the traits that contribute to being an effective leader.

These traits can be communicated to staff by:

- Promoting a congenial and respectful atmosphere
- Maximizing opportunities for the organization and *all* staff
- Learning staffs' strengths and challenges
- Endeavoring to bring out the best in others
- Providing reliable and consistent support

- Giving individuals the benefit of the doubt
- Paying attention and listening
- Thinking before speaking and acting
- Having a sense of humor while not taking oneself too seriously
- Looking on the bright side

Perhaps the most important way a supervisor can empower staff is to cultivate an organizational atmosphere that values open communication, support, and mutual respect. In practice, envision the ideal workplace and strive to be the supervisor whom you would like to have. Reflect on supervisors or managers who may have been less than ideal, think of ways you would change their behaviors, and model your vision of an ideal boss. It may seem obvious, but it is important to remember and understand that not everyone has the same strengths. Different staff members will react to different types of motivators (discussed in more detail in chapter 4), and to different styles of management. Take the time to get to know your staff and strive to maximize their potential by nurturing their unique gifts. Encourage calculated risk taking and allow space for staff to take chances. In addition, do not ask a staff member to perform a task that you are not willing to do yourself. When possible and where feasible, make allowances for individual staff members' unique challenges.

During interactions with staff, keep in mind the recommended praise-to-criticism ratio. Generally speaking, it takes five positive remarks to balance the effect of one negative remark (Baumeister 2001). Additionally, with negative emotions, information tends to be processed more thoroughly, so given a natural tendency to fixate on critical comments, most people can only take in one negative comment at a time (Tugend 2012).

One early morning during my tenure as a public library director, I was sitting at my desk and the circulation desk manager came in with a long list of problems, which she forlornly recited in detail. There was an issue with the heating system, the water fountain was leaking, the interlibrary loan delivery was late, the circulation assistant called in sick . . . the list went on, as she delivered it to me in a resigned and frustrated manner. When she got to the end, I said gently, "Good morning, Ann." I wanted to remind her that we should start our morning routine with a greeting, rather than a list of issues that needed to be resolved. She paused, then smiled and said warmly, "Good morning." Every day for years thereafter, she greeted me and all the other staff with a hearty salutation before diving into the issues of the day.

PROCEDURAL PREDICTABILITY

While in some circumstances uncertainty can instill a certain sense of excitement or possibility, it can have the opposite effect when it comes to operationalization of staff support. In other words, staff members should have a clear sense of what is expected, as well as what is unacceptable behavior in the workplace. Clearly defined plans, policies, and procedures can go a long way toward ensuring everyone in the organization is on the same page. In general, a policy is a written statement that sets conditions and describes how situations are handled, while procedures are the systematic descriptions of how policies will be carried out by staff. Policies should be recorded (with dates clearly documented for adoption, revision, and review), easily accessible to everyone in the organization, applied objectively, and enforced consistently. They should also be reviewed regularly and have a mechanism for appeal, if needed. Like plans (discussed in chapter 2), policies can help to define the organizational approach, enable fulfillment of organizational goals, and provide a framework and template for guidelines and procedures.

Consider turning the chore of reviewing and updating policies into a team-building activity:

- Have staff members work in pairs or small groups to locate what they consider stellar examples of a specific policy, as well as examples of policies that fall short or are inadequate.
- Then have them give an informal presentation of the examples to each other at a staff meeting, making justifications for their choices.
- Compare the policies they find with the library's current policy, and identify areas that may need improvement.

Clear documentation of all types is essential for a smooth-running organization. For example, with the processes of recruiting and hiring, well-spelled-out job descriptions can ensure consistency and fairness (addressed in chapter 3). All types of communication, written, spoken, and otherwise, should be clear as well. Assure that staff have opportunities to engage in organizational processes and are encouraged to give input. Do this by keeping an open door (quite literally) and a comfortable place for individuals to perch when they do visit the office or workspace. Respond to requests for assistance in a timely fashion. Inasmuch as is possible, keep staff apprised of plans, changes, and visions. Remember to keep them in the loop and solicit their input regularly along the way.

Consistency is a key component of predictability in the workplace and is another important factor in fostering trust across the organization. As it is part of human nature and interaction to gravitate toward some individuals more than others, policies can inculcate fairness and help to reduce favoritism. I once heard a supervisor boast they were sure they were effective because every staff member in the organization thought they were the supervisor's "favorite." They ascribed this success to the continuous use of consistent policies, procedures, guidelines, objective feedback, and appropriate praise, when warranted, across the board. This approach seems to be the antithesis of employing favoritism (a destructive employment practice at best); every staff member felt highly valued by their supervisor. Templates and procedural guides can aid immensely when unpleasant tasks are necessary as well, such as initiating progressive discipline procedures. Supervisors and staff alike benefit from having clearly documented expectations with guidelines and policies that support consistent procedural implementation.

EVER-CHANGING CHALLENGES

As access to information in wide varieties of formats increases, libraries and library staffs' responsibilities are changing and expanding, while at the same time, demand for traditional services continues. Priority areas still include responsiveness to constituents and responsibility for collection development, management, and preservation of resources, however. In the academic setting, this may translate to assistance with ensuring student success, facilitating research support and providing faculty services while creating an infrastructure to collect, process, and preserve born-digital resources.

In all types of libraries, staff are still being tasked with responding to patrons' needs for accessing and using information effectively. The case of health information and public libraries provides just one example of the changes increased access to information has instilled. Not very long ago public library staff shied away from assisting patrons with health reference questions, due to concerns such as discomfort, lack of experience, legal liability, and privacy issues (Smith 2015). Now, with an exponential increase in access to all types of health information, health reference is a common service in many public libraries. The Free Library of Philadelphia reports that 34 percent of individuals who made visits to the library were looking for health information (Monaghan 2016).

Health programming and health promotion are also becoming increasingly common activities across public libraries (Flaherty and Miller 2016). Some libraries are partnering with their local public health departments to embed public health nurses, who provide a variety of services, including health assessments, first aid, and flu vaccines on-site (Feingold and Malkin 2014).

When the Patient Protection and Affordable Care Act (2010) was passed, public libraries were identified as a primary resource for individuals who might require assistance with signing up for health insurance (Flaherty 2015). New technologies and resources will always require staff to evolve and adapt. For instance, maker spaces are introducing a variety of opportunities to explore creating "information" in seemingly countless ways. What will remain constant is the need for libraries and library staff to identify, adapt, and respond to ever-changing community needs in a seamless fashion.

IN CLOSING

Ask a supervisor or manager in any organizational setting, and they will likely report the most rewarding, the most challenging, and the most time-consuming aspects of their day-to-day job activities are related to personnel and staff issues. When staff are content and fulfilled, it follows that work processes flow more smoothly and the workplace is more pleasant and productive. While we cannot assure predictability or that there will not be bumps in the road, we can create and rely upon structures and procedures that outline expectations in order to maximize staff inspiration, satisfaction, and performance.

An environment that supports staff development can ensure a proactive rather than reactive workplace and workforce. Flexibility and adaptability are not only important skills for effective supervisors to model, but they are also important organizational characteristics that libraries have exhibited throughout their existence. An organization that clearly demonstrates a commitment to investing in staff will be at a distinct advantage, no matter the myriad challenges in adaptation or expansion in services, or the particular library setting.

BIBLIOGRAPHY

Baumeister, Roy F., Ellen Bratslavsky, Catrin Finkenauer, and Kathleen D. Vohs. 2001. "Bad Is Stronger than Good." *Review of General Psychology* 5 (4): 323–370.
Cabell, James Branch. 1926. *The Silver Stallion: A Comedy of Redemption.* New York: McBride.
Feingold, Susanna K. and Kathleen B. Malkin. 2014. "A Library, A Nurse, and Good Health." *Computers Informatics Nursing* 32 (12): 559–561.
Flaherty, Mary Grace. 2015. "Health Information Resource Provision in the Public Library Setting." In *Meeting Health Information Needs Outside of Healthcare: Opportunities and Challenges,* 97–113. Waltham, MA: Chandos Publishing.

Flaherty, Mary Grace and David Miller. 2016. "Rural Public Libraries as Community Change Agents: Opportunities for Health Promotion." *Journal of Education for Library and Information Science* 57 (2): 143–150.

"John Quincy Adams." BrainyQuote.com, Xplore Inc., accessed November 3, 2016, https://www.brainyquote.com/quotes/quotes/j/johnquincy386752.html.

"John Wooden." The Quotable Coach, accessed November 3, 2016, http://www.thequotablecoach.com/powerful-leadership/.

Monaghan, Elizabeth Michaelson. 2016. "The Library Is In." *Library Journal* 141 (16): 28.

Patient Protection and Affordable Care Act of 2010, Pub. L. No. 111-148.

Smith, Catherine Arnott. 2015. "Medical Information for the Consumer before the World Wide Web." In *Meeting Health Information Needs Outside of Healthcare: Opportunities and Challenges*, 41–73. Waltham, MA: Chandos Publishing.

Tugend, Alina. "Praise Is Fleeting, but Brickbats We Recall." *New York Times*, March 23, 2012. http://www.nytimes.com/2012/03/24/your-money/why-people-remember-negative-events-more-than-positive-ones.html.

Chapter Two

Staffing and Organizational Planning

"You manage things; you lead people."

—Rear Admiral Grace Hopper

"Make sure everybody in the company has great opportunities, has a meaningful impact, and is contributing to the good of society."

—Larry Page

"Being a great place to work is the difference between being a good company and a great company."

—Brian Kristofek

The library and information science profession offers a wide variety of settings and engenders a wide array of opportunities for highly fulfilling careers and employment endeavors. As libraries of all types transform and become "less about what they have for people and more about what they do for and with people," library professionals are increasingly involved in promoting individual opportunities and community progress (American Library Association 2016, p. 5). Five key areas where academic, school, public, and special libraries contribute societally have been identified: education, employment, entrepreneurship, empowerment, and engagement (ALA 2016). As libraries transform, new job responsibilities are inevitable. For instance, many academic librarians are becoming involved in data analytics and management, geospatial information, digital archives, and information security; and in schools, librarians are leading the way in digital integration and providing blended teaching activities in their settings (ALA 2016).

While we can't know what the future will bring, we can anticipate and plan for likely changes in order to remain relevant to our constituencies, no matter the organizational setting. This chapter covers planning with regard to staffing issues, including organizational capacity assessment, identifying and responding to your user communities, short- and long-range planning, job descriptions, succession planning, and cross-training.

PLANNING FOR SUCCESS

Why do we plan? Simply put, we plan to know where we are going, and to get to where we want to go. It goes without saying that any type of organizational plan should be born out of and reflect the institution's mission and vision statements. There are a number of approaches to planning, and many elements to consider. For instance, the proactive library manager will likely be working with a number of planning initiatives simultaneously; generally speaking, these might include:

- The strategic plan (covers a longer time period, two to five years)
- The tactical plan (six months to two years)
- The operational plan (one day to one year)

The primary areas to consider in these main categories of planning are organizational goals for service, resource management, and administrative direction. Planning for staffing lies in all of these goal areas.

LAYING THE GROUNDWORK: ORGANIZATIONAL CAPACITY ASSESSMENT

No matter if you are the director of a small public library, a large university library, or a solo librarian in a division of a corporate information center, it is likely the library will exist within a larger structure and will be responding to a variety of constituents' needs. A logical starting point for assessing where things stand, and how the library can maximize its influence and relevancy, is to take a step back and examine its organizational capacity. Organizational capacity is the ability of an organization to use resources effectively to fulfill its mission (Eisinger 2002; Sharpe 2006). Though assessment of organizational capacity has been used more extensively in the nonprofit sector, Carrigan (2015) provides a compelling account of how the executive director of the Lexington, Kentucky, Public Library (Ann Hammond) used the concepts of organizational capacity to revive an organization after the previous director had been dismissed. Hammond started with capacity building and organizational structure by asking, were the right people in the right jobs? She looked at organizational development—did staff know what their job expectations were? Did they have proper support and training? And she looked at organizational culture—did staff operate as a team and feel valued? (Carrigan 2015).

There are free, readily available aids to get started on such an assessment. One such tool, that could easily be adapted to any type of library, is available online: the McKinsey Capacity Assessment Grid (http://www.vppartners.org/sites/default/files/reports/assessment.pdf). The grid, a continuum, is meant to be used as a starting point and addresses seven key organizational areas in detail: aspirations, strategy, skills, human resources, systems and infrastructure, structure, and culture. If the library is situated within a larger organizational hierarchy, the tool could also be effectively used to identify assets and opportunities for improvement within the parent organization. If you are at a starting or turning point, involving staff members in an organizational capacity assessment can serve as an effective tool to get the planning ball rolling.

Staffing Plans

Planning for staffing helps to ensure there are enough people with the right skills for optimal organizational function. It is not only about hiring, but includes retention, hiring from within the organization, staff moving within the organization, and staff leaving the organization. There are distinct advantages to creating a staffing plan. These include making informed hiring decisions and the ability to take advantage of opportunities that arise unexpectedly. If you are in the position of creating a staffing plan, be as inclusive as possible. Collect input from current staff, oversight committees, board members, and other key stakeholders. As with all types of plans, staffing plans are not static; review the plan periodically and make any necessary adjustments due to changing priorities and circumstances.

The first step in the plan is to identify current staffing needs and how they are being met. Peabody (2011) suggests creating a table with the following categories to initiate the process:

- Function (e.g., circulation desk manager)
- Hours/week

- Primary person (responsible for function presently—e.g., board member, volunteer, staff, consultant, no one)
- Relative importance
  ○ Critical—tasks tied to fulfilling the organization's mission
  ○ Organization support—tasks necessary for the library to function
  ○ Important—tasks not covered in other categories
- Estimated cost (include wage, benefits, office space, operating funds, etc.)

The next step is to identify where staff might be needed, and functions that might be combined. Again, Peabody (2011) gives us categories to create a table:

- Related functions (functions that require a similar skill set, based on first table)
- Hours/week
- Supervisor for the position
- Added cost to organization
- Advantages to organization (include here cost savings, if any)
- Priority ranking

Spelling out staff functions, ranking their importance, and calculating costs to the organization will help to clarify where any changes or adaptations can or should be made.

Another approach to staffing plans is to consider demand and supply. The State of Washington Human Resources Division (2012) outlines this approach. First, identify the number of staff needed to perform the organization's functions optimally. For this demand side of the equation, consider the staffing level needed for core functions, the regular turnover rate, anticipated retirements, and knowledge or skill loss (if staff don't receive regular training). The supply side identifies who will be available to fulfill the needs. This includes internal availability (e.g., are there staff who can be promoted?); external availability; future labor supply; and current training and development. Once the demand and supply forecasts are completed, identify any gaps and see where changes are necessary, ideally combining the demand- and supply-side strategies below.

The demand-side strategies generally help to reduce numbers of positions and include retention, reorganization, work process redesign, and improving individual productivity. Supply-side strategies include recruitment, modified qualifications, workforce development, training, and succession planning (State of Washington 2012).

Responding to User Communities

Libraries of all types exist to serve their users, so planning for staffing needs will be intertwined with understanding and anticipating the needs of the library's community. Each library has a set of core services and a core set of regular users, both on-site and via remote access. In the public library setting, those core users may be a group of parents who attend weekly storytime programs, retirees who use the facility as a meeting place to discuss local news, teens who congregate in the maker space, or homeschoolers who rely upon interlibrary loan resources. In the academic setting, it will likely be faculty and students. In special library settings, it may be a group of researchers working on a specific drug, project, or intervention. In the health sciences setting, it may be concerned parents seeking out information on a child's condition or clinicians' staff scrambling to find diagnostic information for their supervisor before a consultation ends.

While it is vital to remain responsive to the library's core users, it is also important to identify, determine, and adapt services in order to reach out to potential and future users. Are there ways to expand the user base? Are there new services to adopt and provide? Have the core services shifted or are they decreasing or increasing? Are there staffing considerations in such an expansion? Perhaps more staff need to be hired, or staff may need training to fulfill new roles. Examine your user statistics and ask frontline staff if there are groups you seem to be missing or excluding. If your users are mostly remote or in a closed network, ask your IT specialist if they can identify which member constituents (by department or location, e.g., lawyers, doctors, academics) are not using your resources.

Go out in the wider community and ask non-users why they don't use the library; be ready to respond with a commitment of resources where appropriate. For example, as a public library director, attend local chamber of commerce meetings: ask if attendees are library users; if not, ask why. It may be that the library already has resources that community members could benefit from, such as workshops to aid entrepreneurs with creating business plans. Public forums and meetings are great opportunities to promote the library and its resources. In the academic setting, a relatively easy way to become engaged in the wider university or college setting is to volunteer to serve on committees.

Examine census projections; is it likely you will need to add English as a Second Language support for new immigrants? If you are the director of the undergraduate library, attend orientation and ask students what resources and programs they expect from the library. Are there new student initiatives that need support? If you work in a hospital library, ask health care staff how you can supply their information needs; perhaps you can offer lunchtime programs that fulfill continuing medical education requirements. Keep in contact with your primary and potential user bases; don't allow the library to operate in a vacuum. In academic settings, encourage staff to attend departmental faculty meetings and presentations. Establish and maintain relationships with your community, so that you are aware of current projects, can anticipate informational needs, and respond with appropriate support.

Short-Range and Long-Range Planning

There is a plethora of literature available on ways to approach planning within organizations, much of it geared toward nonprofits. As planning is an ongoing process, if a plan of any type is created or adopted, it should be reviewed and adapted regularly. In general, long-range planning involves a strategic plan or plans that cover a specified amount of time—for example, a five-year plan. Strategic planning begins with a review of the organization's mission and goals and outlines action steps and the resources needed to achieve those goals. Operational plans, again, generally speaking, encompass a shorter time period, are more detailed, and spell out the steps or tasks needed to carry out the strategic plan.

Mittenthal (2002) provides keys that can help guide an organization in successful strategic planning, and while these tips pertain to strategic planning in general, they can also be applied to planning for staffing needs. The keys that relate to the library setting are highlighted and are listed in the left-hand column of table 2.1. In the middle column are suggestions for implementation, and the right-hand column includes considerations for staff planning.

A number of traditional tools or approaches can be used to inform planning, such as historical data, patterns of usage, and census projections. Change often happens incrementally, however; new services are adopted as a response to user demand. For instance, in some rural public libraries, one can still check out VHS videotapes. This is not because the libraries are "behind the times"; it is because they are responding to their user communities. There are still some patrons who use videocassette recorders (VCRs) as their primary mode for video viewing. When Crum and Cooper (2013) sought to investigate new and emerging roles for biomedical librarians, they were unable to find the "broad snapshot" they were hoping existed, and so conducted their own study to discover what those new roles might entail. They found most biomedical librarians are taking on new roles, such as social media sup

Table 2.1.   Select Keys for Strategic Planning Success

Select Keys from Mittenthal	Implementation Tips	Considerations for Staff Planning
A clear and comprehensive grasp of external opportunities and challenges.	Stay informed. Know your user community and organizational and environmental realities.	What are the organizational priorities and budget realities?
A realistic and comprehensive assessment of organization's strengths and limitations.	Gather information from a broad range of sources and constituencies, including fans, potential users, and non-users.	Where/how can staff strengthen operations? What limitations can be overcome with staff input?
An inclusive approach.	Involve all stakeholders in the process.	Include staff in the planning process.
Learning from best practices.	Keep abreast of the professional literature that pertains to your setting.	Are there new services you can provide, with existing or new staff?
Clear priorities and an implementation plan.	Communicate openly, create actionable objectives.	Involve staff in implementation.
A commitment to change.	Be willing to accept recommendations and to implement.	Lead by example and inspire staff to embrace change.

port, conducting analyses of user experiences, and assisting with authorship issues, with increased collaborations with groups and individuals outside the library (Crum and Cooper 2013).

To be a responsive and anticipatory organization, nurture relationships with the larger community, be at the table no matter the setting, whether it is meetings of the town council, the university oversight committee, or the school board. Take advantage of informal opportunities as well; for instance, a short chat with a faculty member during an elevator ride can be as informative as time spent in a formal meeting.

Open communication within the organization can also aid in the planning process for future needs. Regular performance review meetings (discussed in chapter 6) allow a forum for staff to discuss their goals and future plans. In this way, the engaged supervisor can keep abreast of pending retirements, relocations, and life changes that may directly affect staffing needs.

POOR PLANNING:
OVERLOOKING CENSUS PROJECTIONS

A local public library director tells the story of being offered a beautiful, newly renovated library as a satellite center for service provision within her rural district. She goes on to describe the facility, with state-of-the-art Internet access, beautiful lighting, and abundant space. It just so happens that the space was within a school that was in the process of being closed. The school was stunning, having just been overhauled and renovated through a $2 million tax-funded building project.

Her library already had two branches spread across the rural population they served. Likewise, the local school district had multiple schools. Unfortunately, however, the school district did not utilize the local census data for planning purposes. The newly renovated elementary school was serving an area with a rapidly diminishing child population. In fact, the year after the renovation only two kindergarteners constituted the incoming class, so the school district could not justify operating an elementary school for so few kids. For the librarian, the same logic had to apply, however beautiful and modern that available space might have been. Given the lack of likely users, especially small children and their parents, an important client base, the discord with the census projection made the school site as illogical and non-cost-effective for the library as it was for the school. In concert with the library board, she declined the opportunity.

Professionals and Paraprofessionals

There are many types of positions available in the library setting, broadly categorized into professional and paraprofessional positions. The American Library Association (2015) discusses the challenge of describing and categorizing staff positions that do not require the MLIS degree. The terms *library assistant* or *associate*, *paraprofessional*, *library technician* or *clerk*, *nonprofessional*, *support staff*, and *paralibrarian* are used somewhat interchangeably to describe positions in libraries that do not require a graduate degree. This is somewhat misleading, though, as there is such a wide range of positions that non-MLIS degree holders are occupying. Some manage libraries, some supervise staff; it is very difficult to create one category that could represent all library support staff. Additionally, some of the terms are reportedly found demeaning by some support staff members, especially *nonprofessional*, as it carries the implication of a lack of professionalism on the part of support staff.

There is also the issue, particularly in public libraries, for all of the staff members to be called by the moniker *librarian*, with no attention paid to rank, title, position, or type of degree. Thus the delineation may not exist in the minds of the patrons. This is less likely to happen in academic libraries, given the educational nature of the setting; users generally understand or at least recognize the hierarchical categories linked to graduate-level training. When it comes to planning for the different types of positions, there is not much difference between the categories, other than consideration of issues such as job classifications, rank categorizations, degree requirements, and pay scale that may be linked to varying job responsibilities.

"MR. FIT"

At the beginning of my career, I worked as a circulation clerk at an academic health sciences library, in a setting with just five staff members. Three of the positions were professional librarians: the director, assistant director, and reference librarian. The other two paraprofessional positions included mine and the administrative assistant. There was a markedly structured organizational hierarchy with very clear delineations between the professional and paraprofessional positions. This was pre-Internet, so searching Index Medicus for medical literature was very different than it is now with our current tools and opportunities. One day the very talented and determined reference librarian was stumped by a question she had received from a faculty member. She had spent hours on it, and begrudgingly asked the director for assistance. He looked through some of our reference materials and came up empty-handed. He casually mentioned to me they were looking for information on "Mr. Fit," but they weren't sure to what or whom the acronym referred. I answered, "Could it be the Multiple Risk Factor Intervention Trial?" (Leren, Helgeland, Hjermann, and Holme 1983).

As the circulation clerk, I processed all the new journals and photocopied the table of contents of each to distribute to senior faculty members, so I was aware of new studies and research. It never occurred to the reference librarian that the circulation clerk might be able to help with her seemingly complicated question, but she learned that day not to make assumptions about skill or knowledge based on an individual's position or title. As a consequence, the sharp demarcation between professional and paraprofessional blurred a bit, resulting in a more cordial and harmonious atmosphere in the library from that point forward.

Determining, Requiring, and Analyzing Skill Sets

In some cases, specific skill levels and requirements are stipulated and spelled out by the parent agency, organization, or institutional structure. For example, in New York State, public library staff are civil servants, and as such are required to obtain certification and complete civil service exams that are tailored for their position. If you are relying upon such measures, be sure to look at the currency of skill sets the exams are testing: are they really testing what you need to know about the candidate? If the required exams are outmoded or outdated, endeavor to get involved in keeping them up-to-date. Contact the appropriate oversight agency and work with them to assure the exams match the skills required for the position. Some agencies also require specific verbiage is used when creating a new position; check for any requirements early on to ensure accordance with agency stipulations. If updating the official exam is not an option, but you need to assess computer or some other skills through an additional process, make sure to coordinate with any personnel or civil-service hiring staff and keep good records to justify why your hiring selections may not match the outdated exam rankings.

A good job description is a first step in matching an institution's staff to its mission. Things to include in the job description are expectations of duties; education; experience; and physical and mental requirements. Descriptions must comply with the Americans with Disabilities Act (for details and guidance, see https://www.ada.gov/ada_intro.htm) and the Fair Labor Standards Act (see https://www.dol.gov/whd/regs/compliance/hrg.htm for a reference guide). Check to see if there are any state statutes that must be followed for your setting as well. Review job descriptions regularly; adapt and update as necessary. In some settings an ad-hoc personnel committee can help with the process. In any case, solicit feedback from the governing body or board and get their formal approval before adopting and posting any new positions.

The text box below is a sample job description for the position of University Library Technician-Advanced at the Information and Library Science Library at the University of North Carolina at Chapel Hill.

SAMPLE JOB DESCRIPTION

Essential Skills, Knowledge and Abilities:
The successful candidate will be self-motivated, work collaboratively, and effectively manage multiple priorities in a dynamic team

environment under tight deadlines. Excellent oral and written communication skills are required: a track record of proven managerial skills especially with student assistants plus the ability to remain calm under pressure and courteously respond to library patrons. The selected candidate must be able to multi-task effectively and have a willingness to adapt to changes readily. They should be highly skilled in using MS Office: Word, Excel, Outlook and Access. The person in this position must be able to lift heavy boxes of books of up to forty pounds.

Description of Duties:
The University Library Technician in the Information and Library Science Library supervises the routine operations of this Library. Duties include recruiting, hiring, training and supervising student assistants in the Information and Library Science Library. There is direct responsibility for answering billing, directional and reference questions, training student assistants in circulation, directional assistance, shelving and shelf-reading, processing new materials and other tasks relating to the collections. The position includes maintenance of personnel records, monitoring student payroll funds and tracking biweekly payroll. Other duties include serials and acquisitions tasks, reserves and processing document delivery requests daily.

Specialized tasks include interlibrary loan and the processing of master's papers. Participation in bibliographic instruction or library tours is occasionally required.

The person in this position works closely with the faculty, students and staff in SILS as well as members of the UNC community. Active participation in planning, coordination, and problem solving is the expectation in this environment. Other functions include solving technical and public service issues plus coordination of library/lab schedules, training, and projects with the Information and Library Science Librarian, SILS Director of Technology and the SILS Student Lab Manager. The individual maintains the library web page. Additional duties include but are not limited to tasks that maintain the workflow and keep the library operating efficiently and effectively. Other responsibilities include maintaining contact with staff in Acquisitions, Cataloging, Circulation, Reference, Systems, and other units within the UNC University Libraries to resolve issues in bibliographic records. The person in this position serves as liaison to the SILS office staff to acquire supplies and request maintenance and repair.

Work Schedule:
Monday through Friday, 7:30 AM to 4:30 PM. Temporary schedule changes may be necessary during exams, intersession, holidays, and to cover staff absences.

Minimum Education and Experience: High school diploma or equivalency and two years of experience in library services, office support, or related field; or equivalent combination of training and experience.

Preferred Qualifications: Record of reliability, promptness, and good attendance in previous employment. Prior library experience, particularly supervisory experience and working with students in a higher educational setting. Demonstrated ability to effectively serve the public and maintain harmonious work relationships with public, faculty and staff; detailed knowledge and experience with Innovative Millennium Library software. A detailed familiarity with computers·including Internet experience, database skills and familiarity with a Windows environment plus [digital content management applications] Drupal and CONTENTdm are highly desirable. Other experience includes a general knowledge of UNC departmental library operations and functions, completion of a Bachelor's degree, experience using LARS, and a working knowledge of MARC format, experience with searching bibliographic information in WorldCat and online catalogs. Familiarity with at least one European language is highly desirable, flexibility, ability to meet deadlines and work well under pressure.

To Apply
To apply for SPA positions, use the Office of Human Resources ApplicantWeb online application system, http://www.unc.edu/appweb/step1.html. The ApplicantWeb will guide you through the process of completing your application online. Applicants will be able to create and save applications, resumes and cover letters. Positions are posted on the Library's web page until filled. For more information on application procedures, applicants may contact

Office of Human Resources
University of North Carolina at Chapel Hill
104 Airport Drive, CB #1045
Chapel Hill, NC 27514
(919) 843 2300
An Equal Opportunity Employer

While it may not seem like a top priority in the day-to-day tasks of a busy library manager, job descriptions should be kept up to date to include new skills, expectations, and requirements of positions. Including a review of the job description during regular performance reviews with staff can ensure at least an annual perusal and assessment of its fair representation of duties. In this way, regular updating and tweaking can take place with little effort. At times, it may be necessary to create or rewrite job descriptions. When this occurs, be sure to consult staff members and colleagues for guidance on what should be included. Use examples from other libraries and comparable organizations to aid in the process. The ubiquitous "other duties as assigned" can serve as a placeholder and can allow leeway for motivated staff to stretch and take on new tasks.

In some circumstances, there may be a need to justify a position, whether it is an existing one or one that is being created. Data may be the most effective way to make a compelling argument to the authorizing body. Concrete evidence can make the case of the need for the position. For example, consider the case of hiring another librarian to help in the youth services department. The difference between "we need another youth services librarian" and "we had over fifty children in our two programs every week for the past ten months, with just one librarian on board" is considerable. The data that is already regularly being collected for annual reporting can not only help to drive service provision, but can also be used to guide decision making and to justify changes in personnel and hiring.

In different types of library settings, the position of librarian may be categorized within the organizational structure and hierarchy in variant ways. For example, in the public library setting, the top supervising position might be classified as director, manager, or chief executive officer. The director might answer to an appointed or elected board, or the mayor's office. State library offices might be located within the Department of Education or Cultural Affairs, or a comparable department, such as Natural and Cultural Resources, as in the case of the State Library in North Carolina. In some academic libraries, librarians are faculty members in tenure-track and tenured positions. In other cases, librarians may have teaching responsibilities but be considered staff rather than faculty.

TENURE FOR ACADEMIC LIBRARIANS

Many academic librarians have faculty status, and a large subset of us also have tenure-track positions with rank. At my own university, the library faculty review process is similar to the process in other departments. We follow the university guidelines for faculty tenure and promotion, which ask for contributions in teaching, research, service, and community engagement and are supplemented by the library's guidelines. The challenge is in translating university guidelines to be relevant to our work; the library faculty at my university have thus defined "teaching" as "the provision of library services."

Similar to nine-month teaching faculty, we are typically hired as assistant professors and, until tenure, each year submit a portfolio and narrative for review by a committee of our peers, the department chair (in my library, we have defined this as our three assistant university librarians), and the library dean. As well we have comprehensive reviews at the third and sixth years, the second of which also includes a review by the provost and president. The tenure process can be smooth as silk or anxiety producing and filled with drama and departmental politics (I aspired to the former but ended up some of the latter).

Expectations vary greatly on different campuses. Some academic libraries have clear guidelines, and many emphasize scholarly research and publishing. Other librarians may be evaluated more heavily on teaching and service contributions. This may be one area where librarians experience the tenure process differently than nine-month teaching faculty. New PhDs looking for faculty positions typically pursue tenure-related positions and presume they will research and publish. However, academic librarians can have incredibly successful careers at prestigious universities without ever working at a campus with faculty status for librarians.

Tenure is a controversial issue within librarianship. Indeed, some librarians argue that the MLS isn't adequate for high-level research and that our energies are better focused on service to campus and the profession. Yet many of us with tenure find some real advantages beyond the guaranteed job: equal footing with teaching faculty in university governance; greater support for our own research; access to more funding for research and conference travel; higher expectations and more support for publishing; opportunities for sabbaticals; and, in some cases, especially in a union environment, higher salaries. Tenure also gives additional protection for our academic freedom.

The tenure process, especially when we are encouraged or required to publish in peer-reviewed publications, can also make us better librarians. For example, it's much easier to convince faculty to ask to retain their own copyright when you have yourself negotiated these rights with a publisher. The most significant benefit for me has been access to sabbatical leave, which I applied for at first eligibility. I am spending the 2016–2017 academic year as a Fulbright Scholar in Ethiopia, with full benefits and partial salary from my university. This incredible opportunity would have been more challenging, if not impossible, to pursue without faculty status.

Despite the benefits, I'm not necessarily convinced that tenure is the better system. I know excellent librarians with strong publication records who do not have faculty status. And there are downsides to tenure: faculty governance, including the review process, requires a tremendous amount of time and energy. On my campus, the annual review process happens during the fall, also our busiest time for library instruction and reference. As librarians, we typically work nine to five and lack the flexibility that teaching faculty have, and it can be a challenge to put work tasks aside to focus on research and writing. Some librarians find that tenure functions as golden handcuffs, with salaries and benefits too valuable to leave behind.

Many librarians have written thoughtfully about tenure status. Please consider reading the following if you are interested in learning more:

American Library Association. 2010. *A Guideline for the Appointment, Promotion and Tenure of Academic Librarians*, http://www.ala.org/acrl/standards/promotiontenure.
Fister, Barbara. July 29, 2014. "Should Academic Librarians Have Tenure May Be the Wrong Question." *Inside Higher Ed*, https://www.insidehighered.com/blogs/library-babel-fish/should-academic-librarians-have-tenure-may-be-wrong-question.
Gilman, Todd. January 4, 2008. "Academic Librarians and Rank." *Chronicle of Higher Education*, http://chronicle.com/article/Academic-LibrariansRank/45926/.
Witek, Donna. December 5, 2014. "Academic Librarians as Knowledge Creators." *Journal of Creative Library Practice*, http://creativelibrarypractice.org/2014/12/05/academic-librarians-as-knowledge-creators/.

Joan Petit
Associate Professor and Communications and Outreach Librarian
Portland State University, Oregon

Succession Planning

Succession planning is a proactive strategy that involves developing leaders from within the organization (Nixon 2008). Referred to as "creating the pipeline" (Hawthorne 2011), it encompasses a constellation of activities, including anticipating management changes, creating a plan to identify potential candidates, identifying candidates' knowledge gaps, and providing appropriate training that utilizes assignments and experiences to foster and augment skill sets (Rothwell 2005). Succession planning is focused on preparing potential candidates, giving them what they need to take advantage of future opportunities, rather than grooming specific staff members for specific positions (Hawthorne 2011). The approach has been used in all types of libraries, including special and law libraries (Holcomb 2006; Whitmell 2005).

When the Association of Research Libraries (ARL) identified the need for succession planning, they responded by creating the two-year ARL Research Library Leadership Fellows (RLLF) Program (Webster and Young 2009). The activities include a two-day orientation session, a custom-designed career assessment, leadership coaching, online facilitated discussions, site visits, and strategic issues institutes in which three of the sponsoring libraries host five-day educational sessions on distinctive topics (Webster and Young 2009). The ARL's program has been highly successful and provides a robust template that could be applied to developing leadership continuity in other library settings. More information can be found here: http://www.arl.org/leadership-recruitment/leadership-development/arl-leadership-fellows-program#.V9Ru6SgrLb0.

Cross-Training

As with cross-training in athletics, the goal of cross-training in organizations is to improve overall performance. The practice of cross-training can provide benefits in libraries of all sizes, and as libraries evolve and expand their services it is becoming more essential to embrace and institute it. When it became apparent that cross-training was a necessity at the library at SUNY-Canton (a small technical college in upstate New York), the staff instituted a program there that can serve as a model for other libraries (Wilhelm 2016), using the following steps:

- Assess the need and opportunity for the program.
- Prepare by creating (or updating, if necessary) individual departmental manuals outlining each member's duties and how to perform them.
- Start the training with mission-critical tasks.
  - Every trained professional should be able to perform each department's major responsibilities.
- Allow and plan for time for training to take place.

The time invested in implementing the program will reap dividends and will demonstrate where workflows can be maximized and processes streamlined. If performed with care and planning, cross-training can create redundancy in the system to allow for continuity of services during unexpected hiccups, more flexibility in scheduling, and in the long run, a stronger team and organization.

ANOTHER VOICE HEARD FROM: FINDING OPPORTUNITIES

Unfortunately, the days when libraries could "grow their own librarians" has, for the most part, passed. What do I mean by "grow their own"? This phrase refers to the practice of hiring eager staff; keeping them employed during, and sometimes even helping them finance, their MLIS (MSLS, etc.); and upon graduation, all but guaranteeing them a job as a professional librarian.

The "great librarian retirement" that was predicted, where large numbers of older librarians would retire, leaving all of those jobs vacant, never really materialized. Yes, librarians did retire, but many of their positions were left unfilled, either due to budget concerns or what was seen as an opportunity to reorganize. This along with the large number of small libraries with equally small budgets, and larger libraries with shrinking budgets resulting in less staff, have all contributed to new librarians having a more difficult time getting professional positions within the libraries where they "grew."

I don't mean to paint a gloomy picture. There are still librarian jobs out there. With the growth of maker spaces, community outreach, and electronic resources, the role of the librarian is ever changing. Libraries still play an important role in the careers of information science students and new librarians; they still serve as a launch pad for entry into professional librarianship.

If unable to find librarian jobs right out of graduate school, many new librarians will often take jobs as library assistants or even clerks to gain additional practical library experience and get their foot in the door of the public library world. This situation can be a mutually beneficial one if handled correctly. Libraries benefit by having well-educated and enthusiastic staff on the front lines who understand the greater role of libraries and are wonderful advocates for the organization. New librarians benefit by being provided with expanded opportunities for on-the-job training and are often asked to help develop programs, manage the collection, and assist with community outreach.

So, while librarians might not get to remain in their "home" library throughout their careers, those libraries can still provide opportunities for valuable nurturing of important skills, at the same time growing wonderfully trained librarians who will go out into the world to make positive impacts on the profession as a whole.

S. Rebecca Lubin, MSLS, Head of Branches, Albany Public Library, Albany, New York

Other Considerations

An essential part of having the right organizational structure to match the institutional goals is to have a budget that supports that structure. Such a budget means both the total amount of money is sufficient, and allocations to various parts of the institution are correct. While librarians are used to moving money from print to digital acquisitions and making other changes in purchasing, many are less comfortable reallocating salary budgets. In the era of 3-D printers and virus-infected e-readers, libraries may need to hire IT specialists and allocate more resources to technology staff and initiatives. Likewise, if a website is the main mechanism of service to the community and serves one thousand times more patrons than the reference desk, perhaps the budget should reflect this, in spite of historical tradition, and assure the website is all it can be, even at the expense of closing a reference desk, difficult as it may be to do so.

Making an organizational assessment, ideally in conjunction with a functional audit (another type of assessment that examines what institutional staff and mechanisms achieve and for whom), can help determine if institutional spending matches the mission of the library. It may be that some important things, such as maintaining a website, can be done inexpensively and demand less funds than their relative importance implies. Perhaps other expenditures, such as the salary of an assistant director, are not as easily explained by the services and achievements of the organization. That does not mean you need to cut those expenditures or positions; it just means you need to develop a justification for the expenditure that may affect hard-to-measure factors, such as staff morale or disgruntled patron follow-up and appeasement. Maintaining a visible, proactive, and positive service profile can go a long way toward assuring continued support by constituents.

The act of planning a budget that matches the organizational plan and organizational priorities will help to protect against criticism or threats of cutbacks. Moreover, if the library has already assessed the value of its elements (e.g., the children's librarian, the reference desk, the website, the maintenance of the historical archive room, etc.), it will be well prepared to capitalize on any funding opportunities that arise, be they philanthropists who engage the director in conversation or federal grant opportunities that are announced.

IN CLOSING

As library services and roles are bound to continue evolving at a rapid pace, forecasting future needs and implementing effective responses to address those needs are likely some of the more difficult tasks a manager or supervisor will have to undertake. The results will likely result in great satisfaction for the institution and staff alike. By fostering and keeping connections with constituency members and reaching out to new, potential users, library directors can ensure their organizations remain responsive, relevant, and valuable resources for a broad spectrum of community members, no matter the library setting.

BIBLIOGRAPHY

"27 Best Employment Engagement Quotes." Kevin Kruse, last modified February 9, 2015, accessed October 7, 2016, http://www.kevinkruse.com/employee-engage-ment-quotes/.

"37 Company Culture Quotes That Will Inspire Your Team." Cassie Paton, last modified August 25, 2015, accessed October 7, 2016, https://enplug.com/blog/37-company-culture-quotes-that-will-inspire-your-team.

American Library Association. 2016. *The State of America's Libraries 2016: A Report from the American Library Association.* Kathy S. Rosa, ed., accessed October 31, 2016, http://www.ala.org/news/state-americas-libraries-report-2016.

American Library Association. 2015. "Terminology," Issue Paper no. 8, accessed September 6, 2016, http://www.ala.org/educationcareers/education/3rdcongressonpro/terminologylibrary.

Carrigan, Dennis P. 2015. "Organizational Capacity and the Public Library." *Public Libraries* 54 (3): 24–30.

Crum, Janet A., and I. Diane Cooper. 2013. "Emerging Roles for Biomedical Librarians: A Survey of Current Practice, Challenges, and Changes." *Journal of the Medical Library Association* 101 (4): 278–286.

Eisinger, Peter. 2002. "Organizational Capacity and Organizational Effectiveness among Street-Level Food Assistance Programs." *Nonprofit and Voluntary Sector Quarterly* 31 (1): 115–130.

Hawthorne, Pat. 2011. "Succession Planning and Management: A Key Leadership Responsibility Emerges." *Texas Library Journal* 87 (1): 8–12.

Holcomb, Jean M. 2006. "Succession-Planning Strategies for Law Libraries: Lessons from the Minor Leagues." *Law Library Journal* 98 (2): 433–438.

Leren, Paul, Anders Helgeland, Ingvar Hjermann, and Ingar Holme. 1983. "MRFIT and the Oslo Study." *JAMA* 249 (7): 893–894.

Mittenthal, Richard A. 2002. "Ten Keys to Successful Strategic Planning for Nonprofit and Foundation Leaders." *TCC Group Briefing Paper* 7: 1–50, http://www.ncmainstreetcenter.com/wp-content/uploads/2015/03/Handouts_Lester.pdf.

Nixon, Judith M. 2008. "Growing Your Own Leaders: Succession Planning in Libraries." *Journal of Business & Finance Librarianship* 13 (3): 249–260.

Peabody, Mary. 2011. "Drafting a Staffing Plan for Your Organization." University of Vermont Cooperative Extension, accessed September 9, 2016, https://www.uvm.edu/extension/community/buildingcapacity/pdf/drafting_staffing_plan.pdf.

Rothwell, William J. 2005. *Effective Succession Planning: Ensuring Leadership Continuity and Building Talent from Within.* AMACOM Division of the American Management Association.

Sharpe, Erin K. 2006. "Resources at the Grassroots of Recreation: Organizational Capacity and Quality of Experience in a Community Sport Organization." *Leisure Sciences* 28 (4): 385–401.

State of Washington. Human Resources Division. 2012. "Developing Staffing Plans," accessed September 11, 2016, http://hr.ofm.wa.gov/workforce-data-planning/workforce-planning/developing-staffing-plans.

Webster, Duane E., and DeEtta Jones Young. 2009. "Our Collective Wisdom: Succession Planning and the ARL Research Library Leadership Fellows Program." *Journal of Library Administration* 49 (8): 781–793.

Whitmell, Vicki. 2005. "Workforce and Succession Planning in Special Libraries." *Feliciter* 51 (3): 135–137.

Wilhelm, Cori. 2016. "'That's Not My Job': Developing a Cross-Training Process in an Academic Library." *College & Research Libraries News* 77 (7): 342–346.

Chapter Three

Attracting the Best and Brightest

"The secret of my success is that we have gone to exceptional lengths to hire the best people in the world."

—Steve Jobs

"Hire people who are better than you are, then leave them to get on with it. Look for people who will aim for the remarkable, who will not settle for the routine."

—David Ogilvy

"The competition to hire the best will increase in the years ahead. Companies that give extra flexibility to their employees will have the edge in this area."

—Bill Gates

A successful and thriving organization of any type starts with engaged, motivated, and satisfied employees. The process of finding, hiring, and keeping those individuals can be a challenging one. Dedicating ample time and energy to recruitment of stellar candidates is well worth the effort, however, and reaps tremendous organizational benefits in the long run. This chapter discusses the elements of the hiring process, including:

- Initial recruitment procedures
- Interviewing for success
- Evaluating candidates
- Making an irresistible offer

RECRUITMENT

A proactive manager is always on the lookout for stellar staff, and for opportunities for those staff. Openings might occur due to retirements, staff moving up or on, or creation of new positions. The recruitment process is likely an ongoing venture in a vital organizational environment. Once the organization has determined it is time to fill a position, the hiring process begins. How this is approached will depend on the position and on the size of the organization; for example, if there is a human resources department, they are likely to complete many of the necessary tasks. No matter the circumstances, departmental approach, or responsibility for recruiting, there should be assurance of consistency in the process. Depending on the setting, there are likely legal requirements for the hiring process (e.g., some organizations may require a minimum amount of time for posting the position; some require formal background checks); be sure to review and follow the necessary procedures specific to your institution. Consult with the appropriate departments in your organization early on, before the actual recruiting and interviewing of candidates begins. A consistent and purposeful process will not only help to make things run smoothly, but will also inculcate objectivity to aid in a fair comparison and assessment of all applicants.

RÉSUMÉ BLUNDERS

When a busy manager has a high stack of résumés to cull through, often they will make a first pass to winnow the stack and get the process going. On occasion, I ask my friends and colleagues who are in supervisory positions, "What are the top three résumé blunders you encounter during hiring activities?" Invariably, the top answer is "TYPOS!" This includes a long list of grievances, from font changes and spacing inconsistencies to spelling and grammatical errors, split infinitives, and changes in tense. The second complaint is clutter or too much fluff, such as puffing things up with grandiose descriptions. Related to this complaint is poor layout, which includes a messy or sloppy appearance. Other pet peeves include the use of acronyms and the use of jargon. Another common complaint is vagueness, meaning the use of words that are not descriptive or do not mean much or lack of substantive information. For example, Hometown Public Library does not mean much, but Hometown Public Library, serving 100,000 with a collection of 400,000 and annual circulation of 60,000 with program attendance of 10,000, gives context. Another tip is to avoid a gimmicky format or supplemental materials (e.g., loud colors, decorated envelopes); while these tactics may get initial attention, they may also imply the content of the résumé is not that strong. Seasoned managers use the résumé in the initial culling of candidates. While the résumé may not get someone hired, it does move them to the next step. With that in mind, the résumé should be simple and clean, so it is easy to get a sense of the candidate. As it is the first impression, every consideration should be given for making it the best initial representation of the candidate.

Different library types may target different outlets for advertising; some common resources include the following:

- Word of mouth
  - Share widely.
  - Use the library's social media outlets.
  - Inform your social networks.
  - Ask colleagues to share, and ask them about their favorite resources for advertising positions.
- Organization's website
  - Consider a section for job openings.
  - Update regularly.
- Reaching students and new graduates
  - Contact career resource centers within graduate schools.
  - Send job announcements to recruitment offices.
  - Offer internships and field experience opportunities.
- Conferences
  - Connect with colleagues to spread the word.
  - Use opportunities such as job centers to maximize recruitment reach.
- State library organizations
  - Websites often include links to regional job postings.
- Professional organizations
  - American Library Association JobLIST
  - Association of Research Libraries for Job/Residency/Internship
  - Medical Library Association—"Find a Job" section
  - LISTSERVs for professional organizations also allow for getting the word out.

- Online resources for recruiting
  - ◦ For "Information professionals finding & sharing jobs & job hunting advice!" visit http://inalj.com/.
  - ◦ Networking platforms such as LinkedIn and ResearchGate can be used not only for recruiting, but also for assessing candidates.
  - ◦ For academic positions, the *Chronicle of Higher Education* is a popular tool.

The networking world has expanded enormously, with more access to informal information about individuals than previously imagined. Social media profiles can provide a plethora of information about potential candidates. If you are in the role of mentoring or advising future professionals, impress upon them the lasting effect of items they post on social media, and the potential impact of inappropriate or negative images on future employment prospects. Online communities are vital for staying connected with colleagues and for keeping current with developments in the field. LISTSERVs, such as MEDLIB-L for medical librarians, offer a low-intensity way to be involved in discussions on any variety of issues. This means of "keeping in touch" can be especially important for solo librarians and libraries where there are few professional staff members.

An engaged manager should always be on the lookout for talented individuals, such as through connections at conferences. Keep these individuals on your radar screen, as it could be possible to create a position they could fill through grant opportunities or other unforeseen circumstances. An important component of the recruiting process is getting the word out, starting with how and where positions are advertised. The following text box provides elements to consider for inclusion in advertisements for open positions.

FORMAT FOR JOB ADVERTISEMENT

A review of two dozen current job postings was performed. All of the headings used in the advertisements were recorded, revealing commonalities and some unique aspects. Employing the mindset of a job seeker, the advertisements were assessed on the following elements: did it include eligibility requirements, how to apply, and if it was an appealing place to work. Those elements are described here in a sample format for job posting:

Job Title, Company/Institution
Description of Role
- Should be in bullets or paragraph form.
- Should be a brief description of the role and the work environment it fits within.
- This is a place to articulate the main responsibilities of the role and the corresponding duties.
- This section is also frequently called responsibilities, job functions, or other variations on that theme.

Qualifications
- This section also goes by requirements and/or competencies.
- It is common practice to state this in two sections: minimum and preferred (or base/basic/baseline and ideal/desired).
- The latter category should be qualities that only the "dream" or "perfect" candidate would have, but are not absolutely necessary to perform well in the position and be considered a good candidate.
- If you split this section into two parts, consider adding a line of encouragement to applicants who only possess the minimum requirements.
- This section should list the necessary education, experience, and skills applicants should possess.
- Be careful not to restate the responsibilities verbatim from the role description section.

Salary and Benefits
- Salary is not always explicitly listed, but should always be addressed either with a range and/or with a comment about how it will be determined.
- Benefits are far more likely to be clearly stated and include leave time, health insurance, and more.

How to Apply
- Clear, concise application instructions should include what applicants should send (cover letter, résumé, references, work sample, or just some of these things) in their application.
- They should also mention where or to whom applications should be submitted.

- If applicants must utilize an online portal of some kind to submit their application, provide a link to any instructional guide to the portal.
- It is considerate to provide a point of contact that individuals can liaise with if they have questions about the position.
- If applications must be submitted by a specific date, feature this prominently.
- Consider letting applicants know when review of applications will begin.

Other
- Many job advertisements feature a brief description of their employer, not just the specific office that is hiring.
- State whether international candidates are eligible for this position.
- If candidates will need to pass a background check, drug test, or other similar qualifier, make sure to mention it in the advertisement.

Samantha J. Kaplan, MLIS
Doctoral student
School of Information and Library Science
University of North Carolina at Chapel Hill

The following description from a recent posting by Children's Hospital provides an example of a compelling pitch:

At Boston Children's Hospital, success is measured in patients treated, parents comforted and teams taught. It's in discoveries made, processes perfected, and technology advanced. In major medical breakthroughs and small acts of kindness. And in colleagues who have your back and patients who have your heart. As a teaching hospital of Harvard Medical School, our reach is global and our impact is profound. Join our acclaimed Marketing Department and discover how your talents can change lives. Yours included. (You & Boston Children's & Careers That Matter 2016)

Sometimes opportunities arise that are unexpected, such as unsolicited visits from potential employees. Have on hand generic literature that describes the organization that you can share with any visitor. Include organizational facts, a summary of the area, housing, recreational opportunities, maps, interesting facts, bookmark, library newsletters, and annual reports. It may be that a position will become available, and if a visitor has had a positive encounter at your organization, they will be likely to remember the experience and apply. For job candidates, add the specific job description to the literature and customize the packet for their needs. Include this regularly updated information on your website as well, for any virtual visitors.

Other considerations during the application process include current employees. If there are in-house staff who are applying for a position, use the same process for application and evaluation that is used for the external candidates. Maintain consistency throughout; screen and evaluate applications in the same manner for each and every applicant.

INTENTIONALITY

When it comes to talent acquisition for employers, the talent is everywhere! I don't think it's a matter of where to find the talent as much as what talent is needed to complete your team(s). When career counselors speak to new graduates, we talk about what resources are important. One popular type of resource is sites like "I need a library job" or Lib-Gig.com, as well as career sections on professional development sites where candidates can find out what opportunities are available. But that is only one type of resource for job seekers and employers to use. Another resource is developing your approach to building your network of colleagues who are both in and out of the field. Some people bristle at the idea of "networking," as it seems very calculated, but there is a difference between intentional and calculating, and that difference is your authenticity. Yes, if you are only building your network when YOU are looking for a new opportunity, that comes across as calculating and one sided. However, the relationship building that defines a successful professional network is only going to be successful if it is genuine, and when you are offering as much to the relationship as you are "getting." So as employers think about what type of talent they need to complete their teams, there should be an intentional attempt to create an accurate and detailed job description that allows for the changing nature of the field, including the different types of services necessary and one's comfort level with new technology.

Lori Haight, EdD
Career Service Coordinator
School of Information and Library Science
University of North Carolina at Chapel Hill

THE INTERVIEW PROCESS

As much as possible, try to establish and maintain a consistent approach across interviews as well. Follow the same procedure with each new candidate; this might entail starting with a discussion of job description. The next step might be to describe job expectations, and where they fit within the organization's goals. Use a template and ask the same questions of all the candidates. Take notes; summarize them as soon as you can after the interview is completed, while your memory of the encounter and the details are fresh. Determine ahead of time who will be physically present during the interviews.

Types of Interview Questions

There are a variety of types of questions the interviewer can use to determine a candidate's fit for the position and organization. Using different types of questions will help to uncover and discover different aspects of the candidate's personality. Permission questions demonstrate concern for the candidate and are an effective way to establish a comfortable rapport. An example of a permission question is starting off the interview with "Do you have any questions about the process?" Factual questions are an effective way to obtain objective data on the candidate. "What do you do in your present job?" is an example of a factual question.

Another tack is asking the candidate to describe a situation, sometimes referred to as "tell me about" questions. Asking the candidate to describe a past experience, or a recent task that made them look forward to work, falls into this category. Questions that pertain to emotions, or feeling questions, are another effective approach. An example of a feeling question is "What do you like best (least) about your present job?"

Magic wand questions allow the candidate to speculate or dream and can reveal hopes, expectations, and aspirations. Examples of this type of question include "What would a perfect relationship with your boss be like?" and "In an ideal world, where do you envision yourself in five years?" Follow-up questions, such as "Can you be more specific?" and "Can you tell me more about that?" allow the candidate to elaborate on previous answers. Checking questions allow for clarification; "Is this what you mean?" is an example of a checking question.

No matter the category of question, the interviewer should include challenging open-ended questions relating to the position at hand, such as "What skills do you bring to the job? What was your biggest challenge in a past job, and how did you meet it?" and "How do you get cooperation on a project from people who don't actually report to you?" (Pearlmutter and Nelson 2012).

THE ICE CREAM QUESTION

In one of my positions at an academic medical library, I was responsible for interviewing and hiring graduate students to staff the library in the evenings. Many of the candidates were international students, often older than I was, and almost always visibly nervous about the process. It occurred to me halfway through one of the interviews to inject a pleasant question, something I hoped would calm them and engender a happy thought. I also wanted to use a question that reduced the pressure for finding a "right" answer. So during an interview with a particularly agitated student, I asked, "What is your favorite ice cream flavor?" In that encounter, it worked marvelously. Her face was visibly less stressed, and she smiled as she answered "Vanilla!" Over time, I have used the question in many interview settings, and almost all of the interviewees smile, and then profess their flavor with enthusiasm. I have learned, though, to be more circumspect about this approach and the wide range of responses. Sometimes there are folks who appear to be searching for what they think is the right answer; others might have lactose intolerance, and so the question doesn't always engender pleasant thoughts. Two results of the ice cream question have remained constant, though: the answers are always informative, and the conversation is always enlivened by it.

During the interview, discuss relevant personnel policies. Go over benefits, and let interviewees know if there is a probationary period. Apprise candidates of your time line, remembering that there are things outside of your control to factor in to your estimation (e.g., the application making its way through organizational channels in a timely fashion, board approval, etc.). Ask for references, if they have not already been submitted during the application process, and be diligent in checking *all* of them if you are at all considering hiring the applicant.

Do not ask about personal information. This includes questions such as, "Are you married? Do you have children? Are you planning to have children? Is your spouse a student? Will you be moving when s/he graduates?" (Pearlmutter and Nelson 2012).

Tips for the Actual Interview

- Allow the candidate to do the majority of talking.
  - A good rule of thumb is 70 percent for the interviewee's interaction and 30 percent for the interviewer.
- Ask just one question at a time.
  - Concentrate that one question on only one subject.
- Ask easy questions first.
  - Allow the applicant time to become comfortable.
  - Develop a rapport.
- Record answers.
  - Take notes that will jog your memory.
  - Take note of your observations as well, including impressions and ratings.
- Give the candidate ample time to answer.
  - Ask for more details.
  - Use follow-up questions to clarify answers.
- Ask for descriptions of past behavior in other job situations.
  - Ask for specific examples of how they handled different types of challenges (e.g., problematic patron, coworker, project).
  - Ask for specific examples of successful initiatives (e.g., program they created, process they streamlined).
- Once the interview is under way, alternate between easy and difficult questions.
  - Create and ask about hypothetical situations to flesh out data gathering.
- Close with asking if there is any answer they would like to change.
- Review notes immediately afterward.
  - Fill out rubric for interviewee.
  - If other staff members are involved in the interview, ask for their summaries shortly after the interview takes place.

To instill objectivity into the assessment process, consider creating a rubric. Table 3.1 is an example of a rubric created for evaluating responses during the interview process. Numerical scores could be incorporated by allocating points to each category if preferred.

Involve as many of the other staff members as you can in the process, especially members who will work in close contact with the new hire. Have staff who might not be directly involved in the interviews give the candidate a tour of the facility or of their department, or schedule a casual coffee break where the candidate can meet informally with a number of people. Afterward, ask for their candid assessments of how the candidate might fit in with the

Table 3.1. Rubric for Evaluating Interviewees' Responses

Responses	Evolving	Satisfactory	Exceptional
Clarity	Difficult to understand; disjointed	Organized and clear	Very clear; terms augment explanations
Perceptiveness	Little amplification of points	Nuanced explanation of points	Elaboration of points with varied examples
Focus	Difficult to follow train of thought	Answers apply directly to questions	Makes specific points that demonstrate enhanced understanding
Reflection	Little thoughtfulness	Includes some personal reflections	Appropriate; includes highly relevant reflections
Body language	Exhibits discomfort	Comfortable and prepared	Exudes self-confidence; very composed

organization. This can be done informally, or by using a survey tool, if anonymity is preferred.

EVALUATING CANDIDATES

One of the challenges with the interview process is that everyone involved is likely at their very best. Both parties are invested; managers are "selling" the position and the organization; the candidates are "pitching" themselves. So if there are any reservations about a candidate, remember to take into consideration that you are experiencing their best version. As with assessing interviewees' responses, rubrics can help to make the evaluation process less subjective, more transparent, and timelier (Brannon and Leuzinger 2014).

Use the same form for each of the interviewees, and have all the staff involved in the interviewing process complete the evaluation. Depending on organizational preference and resources, this may be a written form or an online survey. Have a section that asks about level of interaction with the candidate during the process; for example, read résumé or CV; met with candidate; attended job talk; met for lunch; and so on. Determine primary elements or skills required for the position, such as educational background; technical qualifications; prior work experience; administrative experience; leadership ability or potential; communication skills (oral and written); problem-solving skills; and appreciation of diversity. Other elements to consider, depending on the position, include team-building skills, customer service skills, visionary thinking, professional commitment, enthusiasm, knowledge of the organization, and initiative.

Describe how those elements will be determined or scored. Include an opportunity for overall recommendation as well. Create a five-point rating scale, with categories such as exceptional, above average, average, satisfactory, and unsatisfactory, or a three-category scale: exceeds expectations, acceptable, and not acceptable. If preferred, numerical values can be assigned to each category; for example, exceptional=5, above average=4, average=3, satisfactory=2, and unsatisfactory=1. Then create descriptors for each level. Include a section for comments in each category. Table 3.2 is an example of a rubric for evaluating the candidates' problem-solving skills with three categories for assessment.

During the hiring process, carefully consider the candidates' attributes, how they match with the position and duties, and how they will fit in with the existing team. Concentrate on hiring the right person. While you can teach skills, it is difficult to influence an inherently negative attitude or to inculcate interest in the position or organization where there may be none. The following list or attributes to look for in stellar employees has been adapted from Job Monkey (2016), an online employment resource. The ideal candidate should

1. Believe in the organization and its products or services
2. Fit in with the organizational culture
3. Be trustworthy and honest
4. Provide solid references

Table 3.2.   Example of a Rubric for Evaluation of Candidates' Problem-Solving Skills

	Exceeds Expectations	*Acceptable*	*Not Acceptable*
Problem-solving skills	• Identifies issues • Defines problem accurately • Crafts appropriate response • Evidence of troubleshooting capabilities • Description of consequences of solutions • Consideration of alternative solutions	• Identifies issues • Defines problem accurately • Crafts appropriate response	• Unable to identify salient issues • Lack of clarity in explanations • Inappropriate response to issue at hand

5. Have a positive outlook and attitude
6. Be passionate about their work
7. Be able to think out of the box
8. Possess the proper skill sets

TAKE YOUR TIME IF YOU CAN

The old adage "Those who marry in haste, repent at leisure" has been demonstrated to be true in some instances. According to research that followed 168 couples for 13 years, those who had the shortest courtships were less likely to remain married; longer courtships allowed couples to make better-informed and more sound choices (Huston 2009). While hiring an employee is certainly not the same commitment as a marriage, and the process not nearly as lengthy or involved as courtship, we can still take a lesson from the old adage. Even though a vacancy can induce pressure and increase workloads, *try not to hurry during the hiring process*. If you are uncertain about a candidate, consider inviting them for another interview. It is much better to be patient and find the right person for the job than to hire the wrong person, repent, and be required to repeat the process.

MAKING THE OFFER IRRESISTIBLE

Once you have identified the right candidate, it is important to make a compelling offer without delay, if at all possible. Customize your offer for the specific position, but in general for the formal written offer, include the following elements:

- The organization and department
- Job title
- Salary/wage (in salary or hourly rate)
- Whom position reports to (title and name of direct supervisor)
- Work schedule
- Type of position (contract, permanent, probationary, seasonal)
  - Define time periods
- Relevant benefits information
  - Leave time
  - Health insurance
  - Other insurance (life, short-/long-term disability)

- ◦ Moving stipend
- ◦ Other benefits specific to the position and/or the organization
- Expected start date

Discuss the potential for negotiating salary and benefits with pertinent personnel before making the offer. For instance, if there is not any room for salary negotiation, can you offer a flexible schedule in lieu of higher pay? Tailor the offer to the individual and make it clear that you are offering a challenging position that will promote their strengths. Be prepared for a discussion with the candidate. Try to anticipate their concerns so that you can respond in a timely manner. Keep in mind that different individuals may respond differently to types of motivators; these are discussed in more detail in chapter 4.

THE ONE THAT GOT AWAY

I had been the director of a small, public library for about a year when it became clear that the organization could benefit from hiring an assistant director. So we went through the process of creating the position and crafting a job description. We were excited when it came time for the recruitment and hiring process to take place. We did not receive many applications, but one candidate really stood out. She had exceptional qualifications and relevant experience. She lived on the other side of the country, so we conducted a preliminary phone interview (this was before Skype and GoToMeeting, etc.). As we were very impressed with her knowledge and enthusiasm, we decided to fly her out for an in-person interview. Our preliminary expectations were borne out; she was a stellar candidate for the position. We offered her the job and were surprised (not to mention extremely deflated) when she declined. She explained she had visited the local chamber of commerce and had asked about possible employment opportunities in the area for her spouse, who was in law enforcement. When she was told there would be very few opportunities for employment for her spouse, she shifted her job search to another region of the country. It turns out there were opportunities, and openings in nearby communities, unbeknownst to the local chamber office. Once we learned about the misunderstanding, we did communicate, gently, to the chamber staff our disappointment. We also learned to keep them informed when we were hiring for professional positions. Remember that during the recruitment process not everything will be within your control, but do try to leverage your community resources in the best manner possible.

IN CLOSING

It is obvious that motivated and satisfied staff make for a more appealing work environment and organization, for all involved. Taking the time, effort, and energy to find and hire the best and brightest is perhaps the best investment a manager can make in long-term productivity, organizational effectiveness, and overall workplace morale. With patience, proactivity, and a consistent process, the recruiting and hiring process can be a satisfying and enjoyable endeavor.

BIBLIOGRAPHY

Brannon, Sian and Julie Leuzinger. 2014. "Keeping Human Resources Happy: Improving Hiring Processes through the Use of Rubrics." *Library Leadership & Management* 29 (1): 1–10.

"Employer Insights: Nine Secrets to Hiring the Best People." Job Monkey, accessed June 10, 2016, http://www.jobmonkey.com/employer-insights/secrets-to-hiring-best-people/.

"Hiring Leaders, Quotes about Recruiting." Chalre Associates, accessed June 6, 2016, http://www.chalre.com/hiring_managers/recruiting_quotes.htm.

Huston, Ted L. 2009. "What's Love Got to Do with It? Why Some Marriages Succeed and Others Fail." *Personal Relationships* 16 (3): 301–327.

Pearlmutter, Jane and Paul Nelson. 2012. *Small Public Library Management.* Chicago: ALA Editions.

"You & Boston Children's & Careers That Matter." Boston Children's Hospital, accessed May 15, 2016, http://www.childrenshospital.org/career-opportunities/JobDetail?jobId=2258860.

Chapter Four

Staff Engagement: Creating Opportunities

"Engaged employees are in the game for the sake of the game; they believe in the cause of the organization."

—Paul Marciano

"Paychecks can't purchase passion."

—Brad Federman

This chapter discusses the rewarding and the sometimes challenging aspects of staff engagement, interaction, oversight, and supervision. Different types of personal motivation, such as extrinsic and intrinsic, are discussed, and the less obviously positive aspects of staff interaction are covered, including progressive discipline, the appeals process, and exit interviews.

MOTIVATING STAFF

How individuals think about work, and how they value work, may not be constant or homogeneous, but there are some aspects of motivation that may be common. Work provides meaning, allows us to connect with others, and provides opportunities to produce and create. Researchers describe the "IKEA effect," where individuals value items they have created as much as, and even more than, those that were created by experts; they enjoyed the results more because they were responsible for the creation (Norton, Mochon, and Ariely 2012). Other studies have shown that interest in and monitoring of workers' activities can have a positive effect on motivation and effort if they are accompanied with meaning, such as acknowledgment and recognition (Ariely,

45

Kamenica, and Prelec 2008). Work is not just about the product; it is about the process, as well as a sense of accomplishment on the part of the worker.

It is also important to take into account the function of the organizational environment as a social space, and to consider the concomitant social aspects of work itself. Cultivation of an environment where employees feel valued and respected, and have autonomy and discretion in decision making, can increase engagement, infuse satisfaction, and enhance interaction. Encourage socialization through timing of coffee breaks, ad hoc get-togethers, and opportunities for mingling and networking across the organization. Staff who are positively engaged with their work and their coworkers will likely be more positive, happy, and motivated and demonstrate a commitment to the workplace.

In the United States, according to Gallup's "mother of all employee engagement surveys," approximately 70 percent of all workers are either not engaged (52 percent) or are actively disengaged (18 percent) at work (Lipman 2013). This translates to an estimated $450 to $550 billion in lost productivity; further, actively disengaged employees are more likely to have a negative impact on colleagues, to steal, to be absent from work, and to alienate customers (Lipman 2013).

A supervisor who can recognize what drives individual employee motivation, behavior, and satisfaction will have an easier time of engaging staff positively, and thus can enhance fulfillment, productivity, and overall organizational well-being. Depending on individual characteristics and personalities, different staff members will respond to divergent types of motivating forces and factors. These can be very broadly categorized as extrinsic and intrinsic. Of course, it is likely that individual staff members may respond to a combination of these factors. Thus, as with the personality tendencies of extroversion and introversion, motivation can be a bit of a continuum, as depicted in figure 4.1.

Extrinsic Motivators

Extrinsic motivators are external rewards that originate from outside the employee; they may be material or psychological in nature (Brown 2007). In the workplace these might include fortune in the form of wages, bonuses, and benefits; fame in the form of recognition; and praise resulting in external validation. Another type of external motivator is avoiding punishment or adverse outcomes. For example, staff will arrive at work on time so that their pay is not reduced or they will consistently complete projects and meet deadlines so as not to be demoted or skipped over for promotions.

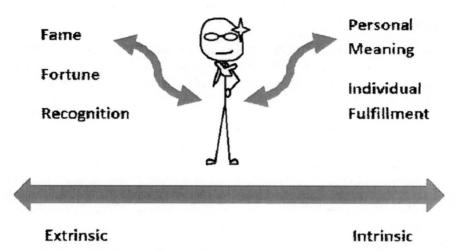

Fame

Fortune

Recognition

Personal
Meaning

Individual
Fulfillment

Extrinsic **Intrinsic**

Figure 4.1.   Motivation Continuum Stick figure: Yael Chartier

With some employees, their motivations will seem obvious, and it will be relatively easy to determine where their priorities lie. With others, it may take time to discover what motivates them. As there are employees who will respond more positively to external motivation, attending to their needs for tangible rewards and recognition will likely result in more productive outcomes for these individuals. Regular and open communication, opportunities for reciprocal feedback, and honest discourse can aid in the process of discovering employees' motivators.

Supervisors should be creative and stay vigilant for identifying and embracing external motivators. In large libraries, employee-of-the-month–type awards are a classic way to provide extrinsic reinforcement at very little or no cost. Varying the employees whose picture is in the newspaper with the summer reading prize winners, having the university president or the mayor mention employees in public addresses, or just highlighting positive employee news at staff meetings can be important ways to engage and appreciate good employees. Activities such as year-end bonuses, opportunities to represent the library at meetings and events, and staff development and training all have costs and the potential for perceived injustices between employees. Thus, what works in one institution may not work in another, due to the range of personalities in any organization. While this challenge may add to the task of being a good supervisor, it also broadens the opportunities to tailor supervision to the unique assets of any given workplace.

Intrinsic Motivators

Individuals who are driven by intrinsic motivation are more likely to find their endeavors personally rewarding and thus perform the work for its own sake, rather than performing work for an external reward. That is, the process of working on the task is in and of itself inherently rewarding. Aspects of intrinsic motivation have been studied extensively in the educational setting in order to better understand how to make learning more enjoyable and interesting; that research can inform our understanding of workplace motivation as well.

Malone and Lepper (1987) developed heuristics for creating instructional environments that promote intrinsic motivation; these can be adapted to the workplace environment. They describe two categories of intrinsic motivation: individual and interpersonal. The individual motivations that can be applied to the workplace include challenge, curiosity, and control. For something to be individually motivating, the challenge should be at an intermediate level of difficulty and include these components: short-term and long-term goals; clear, encouraging, and regular performance feedback; and opportunities to promote self-esteem. To engage an individual's curiosity, activities should be moderately divergent from their current knowledge state. To attend to a person's motivation or need for control, activities should include some degree of choice, contingency, and an ability to exert power over the situation (Malone and Lepper 1987).

The intrinsic motivations that are interpersonally driven include cooperation, competition, and recognition (Malone and Lepper 1987). Cooperation can be induced by dividing the endeavor into interdependent parts; competition can be promoted by creating activities where individuals' actions affect one another; and recognition can be encouraged by providing activities where efforts can be appreciated by others (Malone and Lepper 1987).

When supervisors recognize the primary ways employees are motivated, they can act accordingly. For instance, an extrinsically motivated employee may respond more favorably to tangible rewards, such as increased pay, while the intrinsically motivated employee may respond more favorably to a project that involves working within a cooperative team.

THE WHITE ELEPHANT

As I look back over my experiences in varied library and work settings, I realize that all of the organizations where I have been employed strove to provide extracurricular activities to enhance employee morale and staff interaction. Whether it was an annual holiday dinner to one of the finest restaurants in town, dinner theater to celebrate a successful building project, a bowling party chosen by a staff member to mark her thirty-fifth work anniversary, a day at a state park for canoeing and hiking, or airplane rides to instill enthusiasm for the celebration of one hundred years of flight programming at the public library, there were commonalities among them all. Always, at first, staff were reluctant to sacrifice their valuable free time to engage in "work"-related activities outside of the workplace. But afterward, there were invariably positive outcomes. Staff often interacted more casually and comfortably, and morale was visibly higher after the activities.

My favorite example of instilling morale through such extracurricular activities is the "white elephant" gift exchange that took place at an organizational annual holiday party. It was the classic approach, where you bring some type of gag gift (the price limit was set at $10), and everyone picks a number. Each person has an opportunity, in turn, to choose a wrapped gift from the pile, or to take the gift from someone who has already chosen and opened a gift. In this case, many staff members took the challenge quite seriously and spent the entire year trolling yard sales and thrift shops, on the lookout for bizarre and unusual items for the exchange. Some of the "gifts" included an Australian TV guide from the 1970s, Elvis lamps, jingle bell socks, and in particular, a very tacky painting that showed up in random offices throughout the year. Though it was never organized or mandatory, this small activity brought laughter and joking throughout the office and boosted morale all through the year. Even after I moved on to a new position in another state, I was regularly invited back to the holiday party and spent a lot of time and happy contemplation on what to bring for the ever-present white elephant gift exchange.

Measuring Staff Engagement

Employee motivation is interconnected and overlaps with an individual's engagement in the workplace. According to the Enterprise Engagement Alliance, there are five key components or "drivers" of employee engagement; these include career development, leadership of the direct supervisor, mission and strategy of the organization, job content, and recognition. The most important of these, or the most influential driver, is widely seen as the employee's working relationship with their direct supervisor (Lipman 2013).

There are many tools and methods for measuring staff engagement, the most common being surveys. Gallup has a proprietary engagement survey, the Q^{12}, based on elements in the workplace that are directly linked to outcomes. SurveyMonkey offers an online survey platform with an employee engagement survey template. Responses can be anonymized if that is preferred. Consider building your own survey, using readily available tools such as Qualtrics or Google Forms (as with the example in chapter 5 of the survey created to determine student interest in professional activities participation).

Questions should be tailored for your organization. Hadjistoyanova (2016) offers a template of nine questions to include in any engagement survey, adapted here:

1. Do you understand the broader organization's strategic goals?
2. Do you know what you should do to help the organization meet its goals?
3. Can you see a link between your work and the organizational goals?
4. Are you proud to be a member of the organization?
5. Do your organization and colleagues inspire you to do your best work?
6. Do your colleagues help you complete your work?
7. Do you have the information necessary to make decisions about your work?
8. Do you have an adequate understanding of informal processes and structures?
9. When something unexpected crops up, do you know where to go to ask for help?

These questions are meant to cover the most common components of employee engagement and can be adapted for a specific organizational setting. For example, question 7 could be modified to say: "How often do you not have the information necessary to make decisions about your work? Can you describe the last situation like this that caused concern for you?" Regular performance review meetings (discussed in chapter 6) are another venue for managers to engage with staff and offer opportunities to informally monitor engagement throughout the year through candid conversation, discussion, and feedback.

Keeping Staff Happy

Research has found that incentives and perks are not as effective for promoting employee well-being as is engagement. In fact, actively disengaged workers report more health problems, and on average, report 2.17 unhealthy days per month as opposed to engaged employees, who report 1.25 unhealthy days on average per month (Harter and Adkins 2015).

In order to promote employee engagement, the effective manager should focus on developing individual staff members' strengths and identifying their preferences for work style, schedule, and so on. For instance, when creative employees are given flexibility in their positions, and a bit of free rein for implementing ideas, they are generally happier, while other employees may need more structure and will respond more positively to guidance and closer supervision. Understanding and nurturing individual talents and propensities helps to engage employees, and in the long run the organization will run more smoothly.

There are simple approaches to team building that may help to foster a collegial environment that promotes workplace engagement. For example, some libraries have a communal puzzle for patrons to work on; consider having a communal puzzle in the staff lunchroom. For those who aren't "puzzlers," find other means for sharing interests. At the public library, provide an opportunity during regular meetings for staff to share their take on the best (or worst) new book or movie they've seen. This will not only help to inform readers' advisory services, but staff will get to know one another a bit better as well. This effort can be worked into a display, with best staff picks, further engaging the staff with the patron community. This approach has the added benefit of drawing out more reticent staff members in an easy, nonthreatening, and congenial manner.

Allow staff to share hobbies; in the public library setting, this could be an opportunity to host a program on the town's historical architecture or soap making. Ask staff members for their ideas on promoting engagement; ask what makes them happy to come to work each day. What is their least favorite aspect of their job? Inasmuch as is possible, rotate schedules and work duties, so that those staff who prefer variety have exposure to a greater blend of activities. Of course, do this with input from staff, clear communication, and plenty of advance warning.

When I was the director of a small public library, we offered health insurance as one of the regular benefits to all of the full-time employees. Those who opted to obtain their insurance elsewhere (e.g., through a spouse's health plan) were given an annual stipend in lieu of coverage. At one of our regular monthly staff meetings, a lively discussion ensued about how to maximize benefits and promote healthy behaviors. One of the staff members suggested a stipend for health pursuits that might not be covered through insurance, such as physical therapy appointments or gym memberships. After doing some research on the positive effects of health promotion and employee well-being in the workplace, I presented the idea to the library board, along with a proposed policy for implementation. They approved the policy and added a line item to the library budget, under staff benefits, with an annual limit for each employee. Staff members who pursued health promotion activities were reimbursed after they submitted a receipt that was approved by the board. Though the benefit was underutilized during my time there, the fact that the board was receptive to staff suggestions, adopted a policy, and approved reimbursement for health promotion activities, all communicated a level of support to staff that was priceless.

Workplace Flexibility

In a recent survey, close to 40 percent of employees stated they wished their employer cared more about their work/life balance; this issue was also listed as the number one way that employers could communicate to employees that they cared about them (Labor of Love 2015). In the same survey, the option for flexible work arrangements was ranked number 1 by almost half of respondents as a benefit they'd like to have at their organization (Labor of Love 2015). The business impacts of workplace flexibility are compelling and have been studied in varied positions, both high- and low-paying jobs. These include increasing the likelihood of retaining talented employees, greater job satisfaction and commitment, higher levels of engagement, lower stress levels, and enhanced financial performance (Richman, Johnson, and Noble 2011).

Many options for flexibility are related to scheduling and location where work is performed. Some common approaches include flextime (employee determines start and end times); compressed workweek (e.g., four ten-hour days/week); telecommuting or teleworking (some time spent performing work outside the office); part-time work; job sharing; and remote work. Working remotely has become a common way that organizations allow for flexibility and is now a possibility in many positions (Richman, Burrus, Buxbaum, Shannon, and Yai n.d.). Some research demonstrates remote workers can have higher levels of engagement while they put in longer hours (Gallup 2013). Of course this may be due to the autonomy engendered by the process, but the outcome is positive nonetheless. There is no "one size fits all" prescription for offering flexibility. Communication with staff is key in order to identify and understand what options to offer and which will have the most

appeal, as it is likely that individual staff members will value and respond to varied options for flexibility differently.

Here are some options that can be used to promote workplace flexibility:

- Ability to work remotely
- Adjustable scheduling
  ◦ Time for pursuing educational goals
  ◦ Allow for individuals' preferences seasonally
- Encouragement to initiate and innovate
- Team projects with shared decision making
- Opportunities for cooperative pursuits across departments

Job Sharing

Job sharing has been described as an arrangement where two individuals share the responsibilities of one full-time position; this includes sharing benefits as well as pay (Brocklebank and Whitehouse 2003). Some models might include split weeks; split days; or one week on, one week off. Advantages of job sharing include responding to staffs' needs for flexibility in terms of time and lifestyle requirements, improving employee retention, and the potential for doubling skills and decision-making capabilities (O'Brien and Hayden 2008). Disadvantages include the need for greater compatibility between staff, increased training and administration requirements, dependence on very strong communication, work continuity issues, and potential for problems when it comes to promotions (O'Brien and Hayden 2008). Practical considerations include an essential need for honesty between staff, willingness to work out problems, and a plan for addressing individual strengths and weaknesses (Brocklebank and Whitehouse 2003).

Job Splitting

Job splitting is another approach to flexible work arrangements and is similar to job sharing, though with less need for coordination between staff members. With job splitting, work tasks and responsibilities are for the most part divided equally; both staff members have distinct duties for which they are responsible (O'Brien and Hayden 2008).

Both job splitting and job sharing can be effective ways to hire or keep talented staff who, due to lifestyle commitments, may not want to work full-time. In both approaches, it is vital to encourage and ensure open lines of communication between management and between staff members. Clear descriptions of job responsibilities and duties can assist in the creation of effective practice guidelines that will inform policies and procedures to make the process run smoothly. While they may not be for everyone, these approaches can open up possibilities for hiring and retaining qualified staff, and for extending the talent pool without a demand for long-term additional or external funding.

Workplace Fun

Workplace fun has been defined as "any social, interpersonal, or task activities at work of a playful or humorous nature which provide an individual with amusement, enjoyment, or pleasure" (Fluegge 2008, p. 5). There is an extensive body of research on the positive effects of fun in the workplace, both on individual employees and on organizational outcomes (Tews, Michel, and Bartlett 2012). Individuals who report greater levels of workplace fun have significantly higher levels of job satisfaction, lower emotional exhaustion, and lower emotional dissonance (Karl, Peluchette, and Harland 2007). Fluegge (2008) found that fun at work affected work performance both directly and indirectly and was positively correlated with employee engagement, creative performance, task performance, positive affect, and organizational citizenship behavior.

Even before hiring, workplace fun has been found to be influential in the recruitment process. In a sample of collegiate job seekers, researchers found workplace fun to be a strong predictor of applicant attraction, and more important than compensation and advancement opportunities. They also found that fun job responsibilities and fun interactions with coworkers were stronger predictors of applicant attraction than were formal fun activities (Tews, Michel, and Bartlett 2012). An organizational environment that enables lighthearted, diverting, and respectful fun will be successful in hiring and in retaining positive and motivated staff, and will be a more enjoyable place for everyone to spend their time and expend their efforts.

When I worked at the public library, April Fools' Day was an occasion to be celebrated. The staff regularly played tricks on each other, and my assistant, Pam, took great pleasure in playing tricks on me. These were lighthearted gestures that often involved our patrons too. There was one year when Pam convinced a local realtor to get in on the joke. She had him phone me up to say that the house that was for sale across the street from the library had been bought by a benefactor and would be donated to us. I fell hook, line, and sinker for the gag and asked for a tour. When he had to come clean and admitted it was a prank, he asked if his library card would be revoked. I assured him that I loved a good joke, and we would make sure his card would *never* expire.

My favorite prank was when Pam convinced me to help her into the external book drop, which was located in the parking lot. She wanted to surprise the circulation desk manager, Ann. Pam came in early, we sneaked out into the parking lot, and she climbed into the large book bin and crouched down. I had misgivings about rolling her in and locking the cabinet, but she assured me she was looking forward to waiting for Ann to collect the items from the cart so that she could surprise her. The book drop was not at all airtight, and Pam was very persuasive. I ardently hoped that none of our community members saw me locking up a staff member in the book drop, as I thought it might be very difficult to explain.

Normally, the first thing Ann would do upon arrival was to take her lunch downstairs to the staff lounge to put it in the refrigerator. She would empty the book drop on her way back. It happened that she had planned to go out for lunch on this day, and so she didn't follow her regular routine. I was hiding in the children's bathroom, the one spot with a window with a clear view of the book drop, waiting for Ann to discover Pam. After fifteen or twenty minutes, I went to check what was taking Ann so long and found her with her cart, making her way to unload the book drop. I scurried back to my post by the window in time to witness the "surprise." Ann opened up the cabinet and in an unflappable and commonplace manner said, "Good morning, Pam. What are you doing in the book drop?" If the prank had been a chemistry experiment, the result would likely have read NR—no reaction. Pam climbed out and concluded that she should have played the trick on another staff member. After thirty-five years at the circulation desk, Ann had seen it all, from streakers and flashers to backpacks full of frogs; so she was very difficult to surprise. The rest of the day the other staff members conjectured about all the funny ways the prank could have played out, such as, what if someone had returned a book while Pam was in there? She could have replied with, "Thank you," while wild rumors about a ghost in the book drop circulated among the community. I admit I had misgivings about the prank, but in the end it provided lighthearted laughter for months, even years later, as we all recalled the time Ann fooled Pam.

Challenging without Overwhelming

A former supervisor of mine had an expression he employed to encourage us when we were learning a new skill or taking on a large project: "Take small bites; then you won't choke." This adage can be applied all too often in the managerial setting. For instance, there is a delicate balance managers have to enact to keep staff involved and motivated, while at the same time ensuring they don't feel overwhelmed, discouraged, or underappreciated. Nudging staff members out of their comfort zone is a delicate process but can pay dividends in the long run. Clear organizational goals and objectives; open communication lines; and regular, objective feedback can maximize staff performance and aid in the process of motivating staff effectively.

THE MORE DEMANDING SIDE OF SUPERVISION

An engaged leader will strive to hire wisely, to identify and nurture staff talents, and to provide opportunities for growth and accomplishment of individual and organizational goals. Even in the best of circumstances, it is likely there will be occasions where a staff member might be better suited to another position or workplace. It may be that their individual pursuits are not in alignment with the organizational mission or goals, there are irreconcilable differences, or they are not suited for the position for which they were hired. When an employee's behavior or performance declines to the point of necessitating supervisory intervention, the process of progressive discipline provides a forum for clearly communicated objectives and expectations and can allow an opportunity for the employee to take corrective action.

Progressive Discipline

Progressive discipline is the process for attending to problematic employee behavior or performance with increasingly serious and successive measures, and allows the employee an opportunity to respond appropriately. The goal of progressive discipline is not to punish the employee, but to change or modify the unacceptable behavior. The process begins with the least severe measure and can escalate to more severe outcomes if the employee does not respond favorably. Individual organizations will have specific policies and procedures for enacting progressive discipline, though generally speaking, the process involves something similar to the sequence of steps depicted in figure 4.2.

Some behaviors that may necessitate progressive discipline include:

- Chronic tardiness or absenteeism
- Unsatisfactory job performance

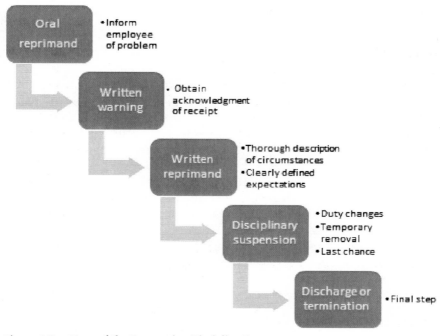

Figure 4.2. Steps of the Progressive Discipline Process

- Inappropriate conduct or behavior
- Leaving the workplace without permission
- Sleeping during work hours
- Dishonesty
- Violation of safety rules or practices
- Conduct that endangers self or others

Each case involving progressive discipline will be situation specific, so while there is a general pattern of steps to follow, a very serious infraction may skip some of the intervening steps. Behaviors that may call for immediate dismissal include:

- Violation of organizational policies
- Falsification of records (e.g., application, personnel, payroll)
- Sexual harassment
- Gross insubordination
- Criminal activity (e.g., theft)

Steps in the Progressive Discipline Process

First, the employee is verbally informed of the issue(s) causing concern. While this meeting is less formal than the steps that follow, it is still important to keep detailed notes and document the conversation. Discuss the problems and give guidance on how to correct those behaviors. For example, if habitual lateness is an issue, the conversation might progress like this: "You have been late on four occasions in the past two weeks; please assure you can arrive at your scheduled time. When you are late, it affects all of the staff members and disrupts the work flow and processes. Maybe you can arrange to leave from home earlier or do errands after work rather than before." Because written notes can so easily be taken more harshly than they are intended, if the written documentation of the conversation includes an e-mail either to the employee or the record, attend to the degree of directness or concern without diluting the core message. For example, the written follow-up to the conversation above might say, "Thanks so much for the reassuring chat today regarding your recent tardiness. I am relieved that this is because of recent unusual circumstances that are now behind you. Please let me know if there is something else I should be doing to assist."

Once this process begins, it is important that the supervisor be extremely vigilant about keeping extensive records of the bad and good performance events that arise. If the tardy employee volunteers to do extra weekend duty or to stay late when coworkers do not arrive, that should be recorded. It is important that the supervisor stays aware of all factors, positive and negative, if they are to engage honestly and empathetically with the employee. If the situation does not improve, the employee then receives a written warning outlining concerns using specific work-related examples, expectations for addressing those concerns, and consequences (see the text box for a template that can be adapted). Acknowledgment of receipt of the written warning (i.e., employee's signature on the memo) should be obtained, and a copy should be kept in the employee's personnel file and shared with the human resources department, if applicable.

If the first written warning does not induce the desired response, a more formal and thorough written reprimand is the next step and should include very explicit, clearly defined expectations; identification of specific areas that need to be addressed; and an explanation of consequences with a time frame for corrective action. Again, acknowledgment of receipt should be obtained. If the problem(s) persists, temporary removal or suspension is the next step. After all attempts at reconciling the problem have been exhausted, the final step is dismissal or termination.

Template for Written Warning

Memorandum

To:

From:

Date:

Subject: Written Warning

| **Include date of previous meeting.** | | **State the problem clearly.** |

We met on (*insert date of oral reprimand*) to discuss your poor work performance, and since that time, there has not been sufficient improvement in any of the areas we discussed. In fact, your performance continues to be unsatisfactory. In the past (*insert time period*), the following problems have been recorded:

List here the infractions with specific and detailed examples.

Include dates, times and description of behavior.

At our (*insert date of oral reprimand*) meeting, we discussed ways to improve your performance, and what constitutes an acceptable level of work for your position.

This memorandum is to notify you that further disciplinary action will follow, up to and including termination, if your work performance does not improve to an acceptable level immediately. If you are able to achieve an acceptable performance level, you are expected to maintain that level. Review of your work will occur on a (*determined time period, e.g. weekly*)

basis, and any problems will be brought to your attention at that time. If you have any questions

regarding this memorandum, please address them to me.

> **Describe consequences and timeline.**

cc: Personnel file; Human resources

Employee's Signature acknowledging receipt: _____

Date: _____

During each step in the process of progressive discipline:

- Ensure you have all the information and facts.
- Clearly identify the problem(s) and use concrete examples.
- Allow the staff member an opportunity to share their side.
- Explain expectations.
- Explain consequences.
- Establish and follow the time frame for corrective actions.
- Be patient and try to maintain equilibrium.
- Document, document, document.

Ideally, the process of progressive discipline should allow the employee an opportunity to correct their behavior and/or to improve their performance. The process can be aided by providing the employee with specific, actionable approaches for improvement that are clearly explained and stipulated at every step, especially in the written reprimand. Although it is time-consuming to implement, if applied judiciously and consistently, progressive discipline can be a very effective management tool.

It bears mentioning that there are cases of managers who avoid the progressive discipline process altogether, and instead choose other ways to address problematic situations with employees. Some use the tack of making work more onerous for the problematic employee (e.g., assigning tasks that are not fulfilling, work shifts or hours that are not convenient), hoping they'll leave of their own accord. While this approach may have appeal for the conflict-avoidant manager, it is inherently cowardly and ineffectual and will only lead to decreased morale and potentially more (possibly larger) problems in the long run.

Appeals Process

In most organizations, if employees feel they have been unjustly treated, they can make an appeal, usually through a well-prescribed process. During the appeals process, the individual making the appeal will be expected to

- Be specific and factual
- Provide justification for the appeal with supporting reasons
- Provide rationale for disagreement
- Rebut any comments they find to be inaccurate

Though the approach may vary in differing settings, there are commonalities that can be applied to ensure employees are treated fairly and justly, such as well-specified procedural instructions or steps to initiate. The following text box is an example of a well-spelled-out, step-by-step policy and procedure for resolving disputes and dealing with appeals via a peer review process from the Rensselaer Polytechnic Institute in Troy, New York.

EXAMPLE OF DISPUTE RESOLUTION AND APPEAL PROCESS FROM THE HUMAN RESOURCES DEPARTMENT, RENSSELAER POLYTECHNIC INSTITUTE, TROY, NEW YORK

900.2 Dispute Resolution and Peer Review Appeal Process

Purpose   To establish a dispute resolution procedure that ensures a fair review and prompt resolution of work-related problems.

Definitions   Confidentiality
All information obtained during the Dispute and Peer Review Appeal Process is considered confidential during and after the process has concluded. All persons involved in the process are expected to maintain confidentiality to safeguard the integrity of the process.

<u>Eligibility</u>

All regular employees below the department director or administrative dean level who have completed their initial period of employment are eligible to participate in the <u>Dispute Resolution and Peer Review Appeal Process</u>.

<u>Exclusions to the Dispute and Peer Review Appeal Process</u>

Concerns regarding pay/compensation, performance appraisals (including unsatisfactory performance and/or attendance), benefits, content and interpretation of Institute policies, establishment of work rules, discrimination including harassment, sexual harassment and matters in litigation are excluded from the Dispute and Peer Review Appeal Process.

Please Note: This dispute and peer review appeal procedure does not apply to employees who believe that they have been subject to unlawful discrimination and/or harassment. Instead, please refer to Human Resources Policy Section 600, Non-Discrimination/Equal Employment Opportunity.

<u>Jurisdiction</u>

Panel jurisdiction is limited to the application of Rensselaer policies, practices, and procedures; however, the panel may recommend changes to the content or application of such. The Vice President for Human Resources or his/her designee reserves the right to determine whether an issue is appropriate for the Dispute and Peer Review Appeal Procedure. The Vice President for Human Resources or his/her designee also reserves the right to:

Determine the appropriate Step for a dispute or appeal; and

Overrule recommendations and determinations at Steps 1, 2 or 3 of the Dispute Resolution Process and the Peer Review Appeal Process that are not in the best interests of the Institute, do not adhere to Institute Policy, federal, state or local labor and employment laws, or do not represent a consistent application of Institute Policy.

Peer Panelist

Volunteer members of the panel are selected by random drawing from a pool of eligible employees and department directors whose responsibility it is to conduct a thorough review and reach a fair decision. Only those employees completing Peer Review Panel training are eligible to serve on the panel. Panelists will volunteer to serve for a two-year term. Panelists may also volunteer for an additional two-year term if they have not participated in three or more appeals. All vice presidents will serve as a panelist on a rotating, case-by-case basis.

Peer Review Panel

A five-member group of selected panelists made up of three peers, one department director and one vice president. A member of the Division of Human Resources will be involved as a non-voting advisor/facilitator for procedure, policy, application of relevant policy, clarity, etc.

Time Limit

Time limits documented in this procedure should be adhered to unless unusual circumstances occur, such as when an appellant has a medical emergency or is out of the office due to approved Paid Time Off (PTO) leave, holiday, or other medical reasons. Dates may be extended by written agreement of the Vice President for Human Resources or designee.

Work-Related Problem

A written statement of complaint, problem or dispute of a situation or condition where the employee does not agree with the immediate supervisor/manager's decision relative to application of Rensselaer policy, practices, procedures or working conditions.

Working Days are defined as weekdays, Monday through Friday. Saturdays, Sundays, designated holidays and days the Institute is closed are excluded.

Policy   It is the policy of Rensselaer to provide a process by which problems and concerns can be resolved through employee participation and shared responsibility without fear of punishment or retaliation.

Rensselaer recognizes that employees possess sufficient ability, skill, knowledge and interest to participate in problem solving and to ensure applicable policies or practices have been followed correctly and fairly.

The problem-solving procedure involves five steps. Problems should be resolved in a timely manner. Therefore, an employee must pursue resolution of a problem within five working days of knowledge of an incident. Pursuing resolution means beginning the process of discussing the problem and providing documentation. Employees failing to meet the time limits waive their right to utilize this problem-solving procedure.

Dispute Resolution Process

Procedure

The supervisor/department manager is expected to consult with the Division of Human Resources during all phases of the Dispute Resolution Process.

Step One

An employee verbally presents his/her grievance to his/her immediate supervisor or department manager within five (5) working days of the incident causing the issue or problem.

The supervisor/department manager will work with the employee to attempt to resolve the situation. If the supervisor/manager and employee are unable to resolve the situation, the manager will decide whether to uphold or deny the employee's grievance by written decision issued within five (5) working days of receiving the employee's grievance. A copy of the Step One written decision is to be simultaneously sent to the Vice President for Human Resources or designee.

Step Two

If an employee is not satisfied with the written decision received at Step One, he/she may contact the Division of Human Resources to appeal to the next higher level of management within three (3) working days of the date of the manager's decision. A representative of the Division of Human Resources will be available to assist the employee in completing the required information. A representative of the Division of Human Resources will attempt to resolve the problem by facilitating a meeting between the employee and the employee's department head within three (3) working days of receipt of the appeal.

The department head is responsible for providing a written decision within five (5) days of the Step Two meeting between the employee and the employee's department head. A copy of the Step Two written decision is to be simultaneously sent to the Vice President for Human Resources or designee.

Step Three

If the employee is satisfied with the written decision received at Step Two, he/she should inform the Division of Human Resources in writing. If the employee is not satisfied with the written decision received at Step Two, he/she must inform the Division of Human Resources in writing of their intent to proceed to Step Three within three (3) working days of the date of the department head's decision.

A representative of the Division of Human Resources will facilitate a meeting with the Division Vice President/Provost/School Dean within ten (10) working days of the employee's written notice to the Division of Human Resources. The Division Vice President/Provost/School Dean is responsible for consulting with the Vice President for Human Resources and providing a written decision to the employee within five (5) working days of the meeting with the employee. A copy of the Step Three written decision is to be simultaneously sent to the Vice President for Human Resources or designee.

Peer Review Appeal Process
Step Four

If an employee is satisfied with the written decision received at Step Three, he/she should inform the Division of Human Resources in writing. If the employee is not satisfied with the written decision received at Step Three, he/she should notify the Division of Human Resources in writing of their intent to proceed to the Peer Review Appeal Process within three (3) working days of the date of the Step Three decision. At that time, the employee will complete the Dispute/Appeal Form. A representative of the Division of Human Resources will facilitate the convening of a panel within five (5) working days of being notified of the employee's appeal.

The Peer Panel will be composed of three employees, one department director, and one vice president. The employees and department director panel members will be selected in a random drawing conducted in the Division of Human Resources. The appellant will draw five names from the eligible Employee Peer Panel pool. Three will be selected to serve on the panel, one will be selected as an alternate and one will be returned to the Employee Peer Panel pool.

The appellant will then draw two names from the eligible department director Peer Panel pool. The appellant will select one to serve on the panel. The remaining one will be used as an alternate. If a situation occurs where the appellant is unfamiliar with someone whose name he/she has drawn, the representative of the Division of Human Resources may provide the panelist's job title, department, service date and a brief summary of their duties. The vice president panelist will be designated by the Human Resources representative.

Please Note: A member of the employee's family or someone in the employee's chain of command may not serve as a panel member. If those names are drawn, they will automatically be disqualified. An employee may not serve as a panelist if he/she has a current problem-resolution pending or if he/she has been named as a witness involved with the work-related problem. Any employee randomly selected to be a panelist, who feels that he/she may not be able to maintain impartiality or objectivity, for whatever reason, should disqualify him or herself by notifying the Division of Human Resources.

The Division of Human Resources will notify panelists of their selection. If the panelist is unable to serve, he/she must respond immediately to the Division of Human Resources so that the alternate may be notified. If less than three panelists from the Peer Panel Pool can serve, the appellant will randomly draw the additional panelists needed from the eligible pool.

Attorneys, outside consultants, current employees (other than those already on the panel) and non-employees will not be allowed to attend or participate in the problem-solving proceedings. Employees called as witnesses by the appellant's supervisor/manager are expected to participate in the hearing process. Failure to adhere to these procedures will disqualify the employee from further participation in the appeal procedures.

The Division of Human Resources will provide copies of the written appeal and prior responses at each step of the process to the Peer Panel, as well as all other materials of information relevant to the proceedings. All written documentation must be returned to the Division of Human Resources.

The panel will interview and gather data only when meeting as a group. No individual investigations will be permitted. The panel will call in order of appearance: the appellant, the appellant's supervisor/manager and any witnesses.

Written questions to be asked of either party or the witnesses by the panel shall be submitted to the Division of Human Resources at least two days before the scheduled hearing date. Only the panel members and a member of the Division of Human Resources will be present during the testimony and deliberations.

After all testimony and evidence have been presented, the panel will deliberate and vote on its recommendation by secret ballot. The final Peer Panel decision will be the result of a simple majority vote. A Division of Human Resources representative will serve as a resource for the Panel, providing clarification of policy. The panel's recommendation may grant the request, deny the request or include modification of the request.

If "modification" of the request is the recommendation reached, additional deliberation and/or votes may be taken to determine exactly how to modify the request. All proceedings will be held privately.

Panelists will sign the recommendation, which will be forwarded to the President or the President's designee. The Division of Human Resources will maintain a record of all notes, documents, minutes and materials pertaining to the problem-solving process in a file separate from the appellant's personnel file. This information is considered Private and Privileged by Rensselaer and will only be disclosed to persons that the Institute considers necessary for reviewing and enforcing any decisions.

Step Five

The vice president panelist and the Division of Human Resources representative are responsible for communicating the panel recommendation in writing to the Vice President for Human Resources or designee within three (3) working days of the recommendation. The Vice President for Human Resources or designee will review the recommendation. The Vice President for Human Resources or designee will make a written decision within five (5) working days of being notified of the panel's recommendation. The written decision of the Vice President for Human Resources or designee is final.

Rensselaer will do its best to adhere to the guidelines set forth in this policy. However, failure of Rensselaer to do so shall not give any employee an independent right to seek redress against Rensselaer for any such failure.

Exit Interviews

Exit interviews are an effective way to gather data from employees who are leaving, regardless of their reasons, and can be extremely valuable for improving supervision, management, or organizational practices. The exit interview can be an informal discussion or a more formal encounter with a questionnaire form for the employee to complete. If the supervisor feels that they have a less-than-ideal relationship with the supervisee, it may be preferable for another individual, such as a human resources manager or board member, to conduct the interview. No matter the approach, the employee should be assured that responses will be kept confidential, and their responses will only be conveyed or reported in aggregate format. Some points to consider for inclusion during the exit interview are listed here:

- Why did you accept employment at the organization?
- Were your job duties discussed during the interview process?
  - Do you feel your job duties matched your job description?
- Were your expectations for your position in line with your experience?
- Were you given adequate training to perform your job?
  - Did you have the tools you needed to succeed?
  - Is there a way training could be improved?
- Were there problems in the organizational environment?
  - Do you have any suggestions for improvement or changes?
- Were you able to work with your supervisor well?
  - Did you have access to your supervisor as needed to perform your job?
  - Did you receive regular and adequate feedback?
  - Were there any specific challenges you encountered you'd like to share?
  - Do you have suggestions for how your supervisor might improve?
- What was the best aspect of working in the organization?
  - Please describe your best day on the job.
- What was your least favorite aspect of working in the organization?
  - Please describe your worst day on the job.
  - Can you suggest any changes?
- What are your reasons for leaving?
- If an acceptable position became available again, would you consider returning?
- Do you have any other unresolved issues, suggestions, or comments?

IN CLOSING

The most rewarding and the most challenging aspects of working in any organization are often directly related to staff interaction. In the library setting, the staff are the primary way by which users engage with the organization. Therefore, staff engagement can have a profound effect on service and overall achievement of organizational goals and objectives. Managers and supervisors who strive to understand how employees are motivated and who work to nurture their staff members' strengths while remaining open, fair, and objective will be most likely to achieve their institution's goals.

BIBLIOGRAPHY

"27 Best Employment Engagement Quotes." Kevin Kruse, last modified February 9, 2015, accessed October 12, 2016, http://www.kevinkruse.com/employee-engagement-quotes/.

Ariely, Dan, Emir Kamenica, and Dražen Prelec. 2008. "Man's Search for Meaning: The Case of Legos." *Journal of Economic Behavior & Organization* 67 (3): 671–677.

"Best Practices in Assessing Employee Engagement." *Enterprise Engagement Alliance, Engagement Strategies Media*, accessed July 18, 2016, http://www.enterpriseengagement.org/articles/content/8304616/best-practices-in-assessing-employee-engagement/.

Brocklebank, Jackie and Heather Whitehouse. 2003. "Job Sharing in Academic Libraries at the Senior Management Level: Experiences of Job Sharing at Deputy and Director Level." *Library Management* 24 (4/5): 243–251.

Brown, Lois V. 2007. *Psychology of Motivation*. New York: Nova Publishers.

Fluegge, Erin Rae. 2008. "Who Put the Fun in Functional? Fun at Work and Its Effects on Job Performance." PhD diss., University of Florida. ProQuest (3322919).

Gallup. July 12, 2013. "Remote Workers Log More Hours and Are Slightly More Engaged," http://www.gallup.com/opinion/gallup/170669/remote-workers-log-hours-slightly-engaged.aspx.

Hadjistoyanova, Iliyana. "The 9 Questions That Should Be in Every Employee Engagement Survey," May 4, 2016, *CEB Blogs*, https://www.cebglobal.com/blogs/the-9-questions-that-should-be-in-every-employee-engagement-survey/.

Harter, Jim and Amy Adkins. December 18, 2015. "Engaged Employees Less Likely to Have Health Problems." *Gallup*, http://www.gallup.com/poll/187865/engaged-employees-less-likely-health-problems.aspx.

Karl, Katherine A., Joy V. Peluchette, and Lynn Harland. 2007. "Is Fun for Everyone? Personality Differences in Healthcare Providers' Attitudes Toward Fun." *Journal of Health and Human Services Administration* 29 (4): 409–447.

"Labor of Love: What Employees Love about Work & Ways to Keep the Spark Alive." 2015. *Virgin Pulse*.

Lipman, Victor. September 23, 2013. "Surprising, Disturbing Facts from the Mother of All Employee Engagement Surveys." *Forbes*, accessed October 7, 2016, http://www.forbes.com/sites/victorlipman/2013/09/23/surprising-disturbing-facts-from-the-mother-of-all-employee-engagement-surveys/#6512c9641218.

Malone, Thomas W. and Mark R. Lepper. 1987. "Making Learning Fun: A Taxonomy of Intrinsic Motivations for Learning." In R. E. Snow and M. J. Farr (Eds.), *Aptitude, Learning, and Instruction: III. Cognitive and Affective Process Analysis.* Hillsdale, NJ: Erlbaum.

Norton, Michael I., Daniel Mochon, and Dan Ariely. 2012. "The IKEA Effect: When Labor Leads to Love." *Journal of Consumer Psychology* 22 (3) (July): 453–460.

O'Brien, Terry and Helen Hayden. 2008. "Flexible Work Practices and the LIS Sector: Balancing the Needs of Work and Life?" *Library Management* 29 (3): 199–228.

Richman, Amy, Arlene Johnson, and Karen Noble. February 2011. "Business Impacts of Flexibility: An Imperative for Expansion," Corporate Voices for Working Families, http://www.wfd.com/PDFS/BusinessImpactsofFlexibility_March2011.pdf.

Richman, Amy, Diane Burrus, Lisa Buxbaum, Laurie Shannon, and Youme Yai. n.d. "Innovative Workplace Flexibility Options for Hourly Workers," Corporate Voices for Working Families, accessed July 14, 2016, http://www.wfd.com/PDFS/Innovative_Workplace_Flexibility_Options_for_Hourly_Workers.pdf.

Tews, Michael J., John W. Michel, and Albert Bartlett. 2012. "The Fundamental Role of Workplace Fun in Applicant Attraction." *Journal of Leadership & Organizational Studies* 19 (1): 105–114.

Chapter Five

Staff Development

"I never teach my pupils; I only attempt to provide the conditions in which they can learn."

—Albert Einstein

"It's all to do with the training: you can do a lot if you're properly trained."

—Elizabeth II, Queen of Great Britain

"The only kind of learning which significantly influences behavior is self-discovered or self-appropriated learning—truth that has been assimilated in experience."

—Carl Rogers

In this chapter, the term *staff development* is more specifically employed to designate and describe activities (e.g., orientation, continuing education, and training) that are dedicated to maintaining, increasing, and expanding staff skills and knowledge. In many instances, the term *professional development* would be used here, but in this case, the broader term is preferred, to be inclusive of all levels of staff.

In dynamic and responsive organizations, staff development is usually a continuous, ongoing process, one that is seamlessly integrated into the overall function and activities of the institution. Opportunities for staff development can be formally structured with dedicated committee oversight and through activities such as reimbursement for continuing education and regular participation in professional conferences. They can also be a bit more informal, such as in-house training at monthly staff meetings, allowance for self-directed online activities, and ad-hoc workshops that are organized internally. Often they are a combination of both formal and informal activities. No matter the approach, continuous staff development is critical for skill retention and advancement, for maintaining high morale, and for ensuring the user community is maximally served.

Formal and informal staff development activities fulfill a number of purposes, including

* Recognition of the need for continuous skill acquisition
* Opportunities for staff to engage in skill improvement
* Communication to staff that they are valued
* Opportunities for team building through engagement with other staff

Additionally, promoting involvement in staff development activities communicates a commitment to

* keeping up with advances in the field
* professional engagement
* staff's professional advancement
* employing best practices in the field
* dynamism and organizational well-being

Depending on the setting, it may be necessary to advocate for your staff development needs and/or to justify staff development activities to administrators or oversight committees. This advocacy can be approached and presented in a variety of manners and may be most persuasively communicated when supplemented by data. From a financial standpoint, cost-effectiveness can be demonstrated by supplying figures for the cost of employee turnover (e.g., recruiting and hiring costs; retraining) for your organization. The cost-benefit of employee morale, and the cost of unhappy staff when it comes to serving patrons and attracting users, may be harder to quantify and elucidate but are no less valuable. Anecdotal data can be highly effectual here. An engaged staff member who has just returned from an invigorating workshop or conference can be invited to give a short summary presentation at the next organizational board meeting, demonstrating the positive impact of staff development activities on employee morale.

Other barriers to employing regular, ongoing staff development activities can include hectic schedules with the need for assuring duty coverage; tight budgets; the presupposition that investment in staff is not worthwhile, as there is likely to be staff turnover; and the unforeseeable hiccups that regularly occur over the course of the day in public service organizations. Nonetheless, these barriers are minimal when measured against the upsides of providing ongoing staff development opportunities, such as how it can aid in attracting, recruiting, and keeping top-notch staff while ensuring exceptional library service and a satisfied user community.

DETERMINING STAFF NEEDS

In order to have an effective plan for providing ongoing opportunities for current staff development, first it is necessary to determine educational and training needs. There are obvious times when staff will require training, such as for orientation, during systems upgrades or changes, or when policy changes result in procedural changes. Responding to these needs is generally straightforward, and training is tailored to the specific task or skill at hand. In other instances, it will be necessary to gather information on what skill sets or knowledge staff may desire or need to acquire. Often in an organizational environment that encourages open communication, engaged staff will make their training needs known to their supervisors. Staff participation in the process is critical; it not only produces a creative climate but empowers staff too (Isberg 2012).

Do not overlook the need for regular staff meetings, not only as opportunities for hosting educational and training activities, but also as opportunities for gathering data and input on staff opinions with regard to skill development and educational needs. Some staff members will be more vocal and will readily identify their needs; be careful to remember to include the staff members who may be less vocal or more reserved about expressing their needs in a group setting. Pay attention to staff's conversations about common issues they are facing. In this way you may be able to determine training needs; for example, discussion about "challenging patrons" may lead to a workshop on effective communication and negotiation strategies. Outside of meetings, an open-door policy can articulate to staff a supervisor's willingness to be accessible and available to staff for their ongoing input as well.

Professional competency guidelines, such as those outlined by the Medical Library Association (MLA) for health sciences librarians, can inform staff development activities (MLA 2015). Staff performance evaluations that are goal and objective based are another way to enable staff to identify what their needs are in terms of training and skills development. As addressed more thoroughly in the chapter that follows this one, it is important to involve staff in the evaluation process and to provide them with an opportunity to engage in self-assessment as part of the performance appraisal process.

Surveys are another low-impact way to gather data on staff's needs and interests. The text box that follows is an example of a simple online survey created by MSLS graduate student Alena Principato in October 2015 at the School of Information and Library Science (SILS) at the University of North Carolina at Chapel Hill to gauge student interest in a variety of professional development activities and events.

SILS SURVEY EXAMPLE

Created and compiled by Alena Principato at the School of Information and Library Science (SILS) at the University of North Carolina at Chapel Hill to gauge student interest in a variety of professional development activities and events.

SILS Library Events Survey

Each year the SILS Library hosts a variety of programs and events for the SILS community, ranging from informal social events to professional development panels and workshops. We are looking for your feedback on what kinds of events would be of most interest to you, as well as your availability for attending events. We highly value your input as we plan our events schedule for this upcoming year!

*Required

In what program are you enrolled?*

- BSIS
- IS Minor
- MSIS
- MSLS
- Ph.D.
- Other: _____

Is this your first year at SILS?*

- Yes
- No

Which of the following areas of library and information science are you most interested in?*

- Academic Libraries
- Archives
- Art libraries
- Corporate Libraries
- Digital Humanities
- Digital Libraries
- E-Resources and Databases
- Federal Libraries
- Law Libraries
- Makerspaces
- Medical Libraries
- Museums
- Music Libraries
- Public Libraries
- Rare Books
- School Libraries
- Special Collections
- Youth Services
- Other: _____

Events

What events would you be interested in attending?*

- Alternative Careers panel
- Author talks
- Casual coffee and tea break
- Flash fiction workshop
- Game Night
- Intro to Graphic Novels presentation
- Makerspace/3D printing presentation

☐ Negotiation skills panel
☐ Short Stories Book Club
☐ Therapy dog
☐ Wikipedia Edit-a-thon
☐ Other: _____

Availability

What times are you available to attend events?*

☐ Monday mornings (8am-12pm)
☐ Monday afternoons (12pm-5pm)
☐ Monday evenings (5pm-8pm)

These same time categories were repeated for each weekday.

Comments (Optional)

Your input helps us improve our programs and events. Thank you for your feedback!

What SILS Library events have you enjoyed in the past? What events would you like us to offer again?

_____

Do you have any ideas for programs or events that we haven't mentioned yet?

_____

If you have not attended many SILS Library events in the past, what would make you more likely to attend?

_____

Anything else you would like us to know:

_____

The survey was deployed using Google Forms, a free tool with an easy-to-use interface. Besides being cost-effective to implement, Forms has a responsive design, so that survey participants can easily access and reply to the survey on a range of desktop and mobile devices. From a survey management perspective, responses are automatically collected and neatly organized, and Forms provides real-time response information and charts. Data can also be imported and analyzed using Sheets, Google's application for creating spreadsheets, as well as Excel.

The survey was administered through the SILS school LISTSERV to all current undergraduate and graduate students. There were 52 respondents; 69 percent were MSLS students. The top first choice for professional development opportunities was the *Alternative Careers Panel*, chosen by 56 percent of all respondents. *Casual Coffee and Tea Break* was included in the top three choices by 67 percent of all respondents. The *Author Talks* option was chosen as the first or second choice by 52 percent of all respondents. The survey

Figure 5.1.   Wordle of SILS Survey Results. Question: Which of the following areas of library and information science are you most interested in?

responses reflect the audience of responders. It makes sense that current students would choose a careers panel as their first choice, and the coffee break was chosen by many as a popular way to engage with classmates and faculty outside of the classroom.

This example is included to demonstrate that collecting data on topic interests of your audience can take minimal effort and yield feedback quickly. Figure 5.1 is an example of one way to communicate data results to your survey participants and community. It is a Wordle of SILS survey results for the question, Which of the following areas of library and information science are you most interested in?

Needs Assessment Case Study: Delaware

In 2012, the Delaware Division of Libraries (DDL) completed an employee satisfaction survey with public library staff throughout the state. The majority of respondents listed professional development as one of their top priorities. To respond to this finding, an extensive training needs assessment (TNA) is currently under way, through a collaborative project between the DDL and the Public Library Policy Steering Committee. The TNA encompasses a series of activities, based on three levels of analysis: organizational, task, and individual.

The step of the TNA most focused on the individual level was an online survey administered during March 2015; the response rate was 62.4 percent and reflected the overall demographics of public library staff. Responses indicated that close to a third of staff had an MLS/MA/MS degree (29 percent) and just over a third had a BA/BS degree (32 percent).

For training content choices, the survey included specific topics based on the Competency Index for the Library Field from WebJunction (Gutsche and Hough 2014). Respondents were also asked to choose their three most urgent training needs. Five core areas were identified by the majority of respondents:

- Cataloging/processing
- Circulation services
- Collection development/management
- Programming
- Reference

These core areas were listed in both the top ten for urgent training needs and for training topics. Training in the use of technology was also a popular choice, including 3-D printing/maker-space devices; digital literacy and e-resources technology; electronic gaming; social networking; software applications; and technology support for staff (del Tufo and McDonough 2015).

According to State Librarian Dr. Annie Norman, the DDL provides professional development for library staff statewide. The results of the extensive TNA will inform their choices and ensure that they are responding to the perceived training needs of the library staff.

OPPORTUNITIES FOR TRAINING AND CONTINUING EDUCATION

Ongoing education is a critical component in assuring high-quality service. According to the recent American Library Association (ALA) Reference and Users Services Association (RUSA) guidelines on providing health and medical reference, "Staff should participate in continuing education and professional development activities to enhance knowledge of resources" (ALA RUSA 2016). There are many avenues to explore and consider when it comes to taking advantage of and/or offering continuing education opportunities, but all should have in common the goal of honing skills and improving knowledge.

If your organization does not already have a policy outlining expectations for continuing education activities and opportunities, work with your administration to create one and have it approved. A formal policy signifies to staff that the organization is committed to their development. The next text box includes a sample policy from the Oak Park, Illinois, public library (2016), which can be adapted for any type of library setting.

SAMPLE CONTINUING EDUCATION POLICY

Oak Park, IL Public Library Continuing Education Policy

Library Board approved November 19, 2013

It is the intent of the policy to encourage continuing education for library employees so that they may keep abreast of new developments in librarianship or other relevant fields and continue to grow in professional and work-related skills. The result of the policy should be the enhancement of job satisfaction for employees and improvement in the quality of library service to residents of Oak Park.

A. FORMAL COURSES

Library employees are encouraged to continue their education through work-related formal courses. The Executive Director will award tuition grants for courses for which credit hours are earned to individuals whose applications have been approved. The awards made during a given year will depend on factors including number of applicants, date of application, and available library funds.

The following will apply in the awarding of tuition grants:

1. Employees who have worked at least one year may apply for a tuition grant.
2. Relevance of the course to the mission of the Library will be considered.
3. Each person receiving a tuition grant must present evidence of satisfactory completion of the course. The employee will refund the amount of the grant to the Library if the course is not completed, unless a waiver of this requirement is granted by the Executive Director.
4. If an employee who has received a tuition grant leaves the Library's employment within six months after completion of a course, the employee will repay the amount of the grant to the Library unless a waiver of this requirement is granted by the Executive Director.

B. ACTIVITIES ATTENDED OUTSIDE THE LIBRARY

Library employees are encouraged to attend workshops, seminars, conferences, or appropriate exhibits. Release time for all programs and library visits requires prior approval by the Executive Director or their designee. Upon returning from the program the employee should submit a written report on meeting content to their supervisor. A copy of this report should also be sent to the Library Office for the employee's personnel file and inclusion in a cumulative continuing education file.

C. ACTIVITIES SPONSORED BY OAK PARK PUBLIC LIBRARY
The Oak Park Public Library will sponsor one professional presentation each year for the benefit of the entire staff at a general staff meeting when the Library is closed. Other presentations may be made two times during library hours so that all employees may attend. One such meeting shall include a "State of the Library" presentation, to include budget explanations for the coming year.

D. LIBRARY BUDGET FOR CONTINUING EDUCATION
A specified amount will be allocated in the Library's budget each year for staff education and travel expense.

E. LEAVE OF ABSENCE
A leave of absence without pay, as stated in the policy manual for a course of study or a special educational project which will benefit the Library may be approved by the Executive Director if library scheduling requirements permit.

F. CONTINUING EDUCATION INFORMATION
Notices of continuing education opportunities and available financial assistance will be routed to all staff.

G. PROFESSIONAL ASSOCIATION MEMBERSHIPS
1. The Library desires to encourage staff to participate in job related membership associations. With approval of the Executive Director or their designee, the Library will pay for one annual membership in such a professional, civic, or community-wide organization for each requesting employee. In general, preference will be given to requests from full time employees. When funds are insufficient to meet all anticipated requests, the Executive Director shall allocate funds at their discretion.

2. The Library will pay for annual membership in the Illinois Library Association and the American Library Association for all members of the Board of Library Trustees.
3. For the Executive Director, the Library will pay annual membership dues in the Illinois Library Association, the American Library Association, Rotary Club, and other community organizations.
4. Other membership dues for the Library will be paid at the discretion of the Executive Director.

After determining staff's training needs, the next step is how to best respond to those needs, given the realities of your organization. For instance, if budgets are tight you may have to rely on using resources at hand. This doesn't have to be limited to internal resources, however. Consider in-house training with local counterparts, such as inviting the local American Red Cross chapter for disaster preparedness planning or CPR training or the local police department to host a workshop on how to deescalate challenging patron situations. Another approach may involve partnering with other local educational service organizations; for example, Literacy Volunteers of America are often looking for volunteers and venues for training. Online resources, such as webinars and MOOCs, offer a wide variety of low-cost training opportunities as well. Include time for staff to engage in training and development in regular scheduling, and always include some type of evaluation or assessment of activities to inform future undertakings.

Cross-training (discussed in chapter 2) can be another cost-effective way to allow staff to broaden and develop skill sets and to encourage team building. There is the added benefit of creating redundancy in the organizational system as well. For instance, if a staff member has to take a prolonged leave of absence, there will be a knowledgeable staff member to help with their duties and who can train others on the tasks.

Obtaining new skills is a primary motivation for staff to engage in training and continuing education initiatives. These can include an array of subjects with numerous, interconnected, and overlapping ways to engage, as depicted in figure 5.2. Please note that these are not meant to represent mutually exclusive categories (e.g., professional associations certainly offer webinars, and workshops can include continuing education credits), but are categorized as such for ease of discussion.

Figure 5.2.   Opportunities for Staff Involvement

- Self-directed learning through online resources
  - A number of libraries have reported implementing this approach effectively with the resources available from WebJunction (Green 2013; Sewell 2014).
  - Webinars are a great and affordable way to offer training (Coiffe 2012) and are available from a variety of providers. For example, the MLA offers on-demand webinars on a wide variety of topics (MLA 2017), and the National Networks of Libraries of Medicine regional offices offer many recorded webinars (National Network of Libraries of Medicine 2016).
  - Open source opportunities are another low-cost approach. Massive open online courses (MOOCs), offered by universities and nonprofits, can be self-paced, allow for unlimited participation, and cover a broad range of topics. Some starting points for identifying MOOCs include www.edx. org; www.mooc.org; www.coursera.org; and www.educause.edu.
  - Lynda.com, now part of the social networking service LinkedIn, also offers (fee-based) opportunities for continuing education on a number of topics relevant to the library profession.

- Workshops
  - As in-house activities, these are a relatively easy and effective way for staff to acquire new skills. Hands-on activities can enliven and add to active participation.
  - There are innumerable opportunities for staff to engage in workshops to sharpen their skills; challenge staff to identify workshops that will enhance their skill sets.
- Professional associations and organizations
  - Local and regional involvement are cost-effective ways for staff to engage in professional development activities (Goldman 2014).
  - Committee membership is another valuable and important way for staff to learn new skills and be exposed to and involved in educational opportunities.
  - Active involvement in professional organizations is especially recommended for solo librarians so that they remain engaged in and are connected to their practitioner community.
- Conferences
  - The benefits of attending conferences are numerous, including increasing current awareness and objectivity, promoting evidence-based practice, new knowledge, and providing networking opportunities (Jenkins 2015).
  - One seasoned professional states, *"I've learned so much more at conferences than I ever did in the classroom; I couldn't do my job without attending conferences."* (Jane Bethel, Electronic Resources/Reference Librarian, EPA Library, Research Triangle Park, North Carolina)
  - Conferences can be particularly important for solo librarians, as they provide opportunities for interacting with vendors, networking with fellow professionals, and developing and honing skills.
- Certificates
  - In general, certification focuses on competencies and minimum standards in specific skill areas. Certificates can be an effective and tangible way for staff to demonstrate command of new knowledge and expertise. Preconference activities and workshops are often an avenue for this type of validation.
  - There are many opportunities for all levels of library staff serving in all types of libraries in this area. For example, for library staff in positions that don't require a graduate degree, the ALA offers the Library Support Staff Certification (LSSC) program, which requires demonstration of competency in six out of ten skill sets related to library management (ALA LSSC 2016).

- Credential and degree programs
  - Opportunities for ongoing credentialing are attractive ways for staff in all types of library settings to engage in the profession. For example, the MLA-sponsored Academy of Health Information Professionals (AHIP) is a credentialing program with varying membership levels. Membership in AHIP demonstrates a commitment to professional development and active participation in the medical library profession. More information is available on the MLA website: http://www.mlanet.org/p/cm/ld/fid=41.
  - Fostering opportunities for library support staff to pursue a graduate library science degree serves to strengthen the profession and workforce. Programs such as Syracuse University's 25 percent tuition awards for library employees and for New York State residents can subsidize staff efforts (Syracuse iSchool 2015). In Delaware, the Division of Libraries offers a loan program with forgiveness options for residents pursuing their graduate LIS degree (Delaware Department of Education 2016). Investigate and actively instigate and support opportunities in your organizations to encourage educational advancement for all levels of staff.
  - For library managers who do not possess an MLIS degree, certification and educational opportunities are also available through ALA's Library Support Staff Certification program: http://www.ala.org/onlinelearning/management/classes/lssc.
- Opportunities for non-MLIS staff
  - Encourage library support staff to join and become involved in organizations as well, such as ALA's Allied Professionals Association arm, http://ala-apa.org/, and the Library Support Staff Interest Round Table (LSSIRT), http://www.ala.org/lssirt/. There are many state-level organizations too; a directory can be found here: http://www.ala.org/lssirt/sites/ala.org.lssirt/files/content/lssirtresources/2011_LSSIRT_Directory.pdf.

Mobile technologies can allow for expanded opportunities for staff development activities and are likely to continue to increase in usage. Tools such as *23 mobile things* can aid in training staff on how to become more adept and comfortable with mobile technology (although the tool is no longer updated regularly, the subjects covered are still current and relevant). In Trinidad and Tobago, a study of school librarians found that the creation of a virtual community of practice had positive effects on social, technical, and cognitive skill sets (Primus 2011). Virtual communities can also allow for opportunities for solo librarians to engage with other practitioners. Encourage staff to explore, take risks, and employ new ways of providing services.

After staff engage in development activities, be sure to have a venue for them to report and reflect upon what they learned—for example, at regular staff meetings. Better yet, have them conduct in-house training where they can share their new skills with other staff. In this way each one can teach one, and keep the cycle going. Another vehicle for maximizing results from professional development may be to have staff summarize what they learned, and then to include their reflection in internal communications and in their personnel file. Figure 5.3 represents the continuous cycle of staff development.

Encouragement of staffs' engagement in research initiatives is another way to inspire and motivate individuals, and to move the library field forward. Nurture staff interests and assist with developing ways to objectively examine and measure results of their efforts. For example, if a new program is initiated, come up with ways to define, measure, and report its success (or ways to improve, if it's not successful). Allow for time and adequate support so that staff can keep abreast of new developments; encourage them to share results of their efforts through professional publishing venues. Consider weekly or monthly lunch sessions where everyone reads a research-based article and

Figure 5.3.   Cycle of Staff Development

shares their thoughts; take turns on suggestions of topics, venues, and who leads the discussion. Endeavor to inculcate a climate of inquiry and examination of ways to improve practice.

MENTORING

Mentorship programs have been shown to lead to increases in worker engagement and employee satisfaction, as well as a decrease in institutional turnover (Harrington and Marshall 2014). As with staff development activities in general, mentoring can also be performed with varying degrees of formality and structure. New employees can be paired with more seasoned professionals to guide them in the early days of their careers. Sometimes mentoring can take place with a broader structure, such as using resource teams where professionals from different departments guide new staff (Bosch, Ramachandran, Luévano, and Wakiji 2010). By sharing information while nurturing new professionals, mentoring programs are an effective way to ensure institutional resilience and memory.

Library associations and organizations are valuable resources for assistance with mentoring. It is worthwhile to encourage your staff to become involved in these organizations, both as mentees and mentors. For solo librarians, having a mentor through a professional organization can help guard against isolation and feeling disconnected. The Medical Library Association (mlanet.org) has a long history of mentorship for professionals at all stages in their careers. They also have extensive guidelines and offer tips on the mentoring process. Some organizations (e.g., the Music Library Association), offer specific mentoring opportunities, such as for conference attendees (Music Library Association 2015).

The American Library Association hosts a number of opportunities for mentors and mentees alike, encouraging participation in the "transformative" experience that the mentor relationship and activities can provide. These include division-, section-, and roundtable-sponsored opportunities, such as those listed below, from their website (http://www.ala.org/transforminglibraries/mentoring-opportunities):

- ACRL Dr. E. J. Josey Mentoring Program for Spectrum Scholars links participating library school students and newly graduated librarians who are of American Indian/Alaska Native, Asian, Black/African American, Hispanic/Latino, or Native Hawaiian/Other Pacific Islander descent with established academic librarians.

- ACRL College Library Directors Mentor Program matches a first-year college library director with an experienced college library director.
- ACRL Instruction Section Mentoring Program contributes to the professional development of academic librarians interested in information literacy instruction and improving their teaching skills by pairing librarians experienced in teaching with librarians new to instruction or to the Instruction Section.
- ALSC Mentoring Program seeks to match individuals with an interest in library service to children. A one-year program, participants have the opportunity to apply twice a year (once in the summer, once in the fall). This program is administered by the ALSC Membership Committee and the Managing Children's Services Committee.
- Gay, Lesbian, Bisexual, and Transgender Round Table Buddy Program pairs an active member of the roundtable with a new or prospective GLB-TRT member, as well as any member becoming active for the first time or after a long absence.
- LLAMA Mentoring Program pairs librarians who are currently in leadership positions with librarians who are interested in becoming leaders.
- New Members Round Table program pairs a more experienced NMRT member with a new ALA member with less than five years' experience as a librarian.
- STS Sci/Tech Library Mentors relationship is typically developed between someone who is new to the profession and a more experienced professional. However, mentoring relationships can involve someone who has been in the field for a while but is changing career paths or someone who is just looking for support and direction.
- YALSA's virtual mentoring program pairs an experienced librarian with a new librarian or graduate student in a library science program.

ALA discussion groups for mentoring include

- IRRT International Librarians' Orientation/Mentoring Committee organizes the orientation for international visitors at the annual conference and works closely with the ALA International Relations Office to develop a mentoring program for the annual conference.
- LLAMA Mentoring Committee plans, implements, and oversees an ongoing LLAMA mentoring program.
- Association of Library Collections and Technical Services Recruitment and Mentoring Committee (Cataloging and Metadata Management Section)
- MentorConnect is an informal mentoring network implemented within ALA Connect that allows all ALA members to participate and only re-

quires that you actively choose to join the network in order to begin serving as a mentor or seeking a mentor.

ALA also lists affiliate mentoring programs, such as

- Black Caucus of ALA
- Council on Library/Media Technicians Bibliography on Mentoring
- REFORMA Mentoring Program

Active mentorship programs include professional and psychosocial benefits for mentees and mentors and can be a powerful tool for staff development and team building.

IN CLOSING

The benefits of offering ongoing, vibrant staff development activities are myriad. They not only communicate to staff that they are valued, but ensure that services stay up-to-date. Everyone in the library organization, from the top down, can gain from engaging in professional development activities, and supervisors should lead by example and be proactive in seeking out, engaging in, and providing access to a wide variety of opportunities. Because the most valuable asset in the library is the team of staff, as we invest in our infrastructure and other resources, we should also invest in their continuous growth and well-being.

SELECTED RESOURCES
FOR STAFF DEVELOPMENT ACTIVITIES

Allan, Barbara. 2013. *The No-Nonsense Guide to Training in Libraries*. London: Facet.

Barwick, Kathryn and Mylee Joseph. 2016. "23Mobilethings—Exploring The Potential of Mobile Tools for Delivering Library Services," *23Mobilethings*, accessed May 24 2016, http://23mobilethings.net/wpress/.

Connor, Elizabeth, ed. 2009. *An Introduction to Staff Development in Academic Libraries*. London: Routledge.

Donovan, Georgie L. and Miguel Figueroa, eds. 2009. *Staff Development Strategies That Work! Stories and Strategies from New Librarians*. New York: Neal-Schuman Publishers.

Kaagan, Stephen S. 2008. *30 Reflective Staff Development Exercises for Educators*. Thousand Oaks, CA: Corwin Press.

Trotta, Marcia. 2011. *Staff Development on a Shoestring: A How-to-Do-It Manual for Librarians*. New York: Neal-Schuman Publishers.

BIBLIOGRAPHY

"Ada Leigh Soles Memorial Professional Librarian and Archivist Incentive Program." Delaware Department of Education Higher Education Office, accessed May 26, 2016, http://www.doe.k12.de.us/Page/1948.

"AHIP Credentialing, Academy of Health Information Professionals." Medical Library Association, accessed May 24, 2016, http://www.mlanet.org/p/cm/ld/fid=41.

Barwick, Kathryn and Mylee Joseph. 2016. "23Mobilethings—Exploring The Potential of Mobile Tools for Delivering Library Services." *23Mobilethings*, accessed May 24, 2016, http://23mobilethings.net/wpress/.

Bosch, Eileen K., Hema Ramachandran, Susan Luévano, and Eileen Wakiji. 2010. "The Resource Team Model: An Innovative Mentoring Program for Academic Librarians." *New Review of Academic Librarianship* 16 (1): 57–74.

Coiffe, Dorothea J. 2012. "Webinars: Continuing Education and Professional Development for Librarians." *Journal of the Library Administration & Management Section* 9 (1): 37–48.

"Conference Mentoring Program." Music Library Association, accessed May 24, 2016, http://www.musiclibraryassoc.org/page/mla_2015_mentors.

"Continuing Education." Oak Park, Illinois, Public Library, accessed May 26, 2016, http://oppl.org/about/policies/continuing-education.

del Tufo, Theresa and Katie McDonough. Delaware Libraries Training Needs Assessment Report: A Collaborative Project between the Delaware Division of Libraries and the Public Library Policy Steering Committee. Dover, DE: Division of Libraries, July 2015.

"Famous Quotes for Training and Development." CiteHR, accessed May 24, 2016, http://www.citehr.com/41401-famous-quotes-training-development.html.

Goldman, Crystal. 2014. "The Benefits of Local Involvement: Professional Development through State and Regional Library Associations." *Practical Academic Librarianship: The International Journal of the SLA Academic Division* 4 (2): i–xi.

Green, Susan. "A Happy Hour for Library Staff Learning." *OCLC WebJunction*, last modified July 13, 2013, accessed June 6, 2016, http://www.webjunction.org/news/webjunction/happy-hour-for-library-staff-learning.html.

Gutsche, Betha and Brenda Hough. "Competency Index for the Library Field 2014." *WebJunction*, last modified March 19, 2015, accessed June 8, 2016, http://www.webjunction.org/documents/webjunction/Competency_Index_for_the_Library_Field.html.

Harrington, Marni R. and Elizabeth Marshall. 2014. "Analyses of Mentoring Expectations, Activities, and Support in Canadian Academic Libraries." *College & Research Libraries* 75 (6): 763–790.

"Health and Medical References Guidelines." American Library Association Reference and User Services Association, accessed May 24, 2016, http://www.ala.org/rusa/resources/guidelines/guidelinesmedical.

Isberg, Catharina. 2012. "Professional Development, Values and Strategy—The Means for Building Strong Libraries for the Future!" *IFLA Journal* 38 (1): 35–36.

Jenkins, Ruth. 2015. "Learning and Teaching in Action." *Health Information & Libraries Journal* 32: 156–160.

"LSSC Home." American Library Association, Library Support Staff Certification, accessed May 26, 2016, http://ala-apa.org/lssc/.

"Mentoring Opportunities | Libraries Transform." American Library Association, accessed May 24, 2016, http://www.ala.org/transforminglibraries/mentoring-opportunities.

"Merit-Based Awards—Master's and Certificate Students." Syracuse University, School of Information Studies, accessed May 23, 2016, http://ischool.syr.edu/admissions/merit-based-awards/.

Primus, Simone J. 2011. "Professional Development of School Library Staff in Trinidad and Tobago." In *International Association of School Librarianship. Selected Papers from the IASL Annual Conference*, p. 1. International Association of School Librarianship.

"Professional Development, Webinars and e-Courses" Medical Library Association, accessed May 7, 2017, http://www.mlanet.org/p/cm/ld/fid=412.

"Professional Development, Find or Become a Mentor." Medical Library Association, accessed May 24, 2016, http://www.mlanet.org/p/cm/ld/fid=45.

"Professional Development, Professional Competencies." Medical Library Association, accessed May 24, 2016, http://www.mlanet.org/p/cm/ld/fid=39.

"Recorded Webinars." National Network of Libraries of Medicine, New England Region, accessed May 24, 2016, http://nnlm.gov/ner/training/distancelearning.html.

Sewell, Sarah. 2014. "A Self-Directed Learning Approach to Staff Professional Development." *Arkansas Library Journal* 71 (4): 4–5.

Chapter Six

Staff Evaluation

"I have yet to find a man, however exalted his station, who did not do better work and put forth greater effort under a spirit of approval than under a spirit of criticism."

—Charles Schwab

"The only man who behaves sensibly is my tailor; he takes my measurements anew every time he sees me, while all the rest go on with their old measurements and expect me to fit them."

—George Bernard Shaw

Regular performance appraisals (also referred to as reviews, assessments, or evaluations) that enable and allow for objective feedback are an important and integral component of staff support. Although historically such appraisals may have been viewed as a punitive process, they can play a positive role in staff empowerment and motivation as well as identify areas for improvement. Though many employees may shudder at the mention of an annual evaluation, an organizational environment that includes regular, ongoing performance-based assessment allows management to work in concert with staff:

- To determine key responsibilities
- To set goals and objectives
- To discuss and mutually agree upon expectations
- To create performance measures
- To identify opportunities for improvement
- To support new skills acquisition

- To record successful efforts
- To document progress
- To celebrate accomplishments

Whether you are joining an organization with an already established routine for performance review and evaluation or are adapting, introducing, or creating a new one, it is imperative to involve staff throughout the process. A clear and transparent communication structure can help to make a process that some staff members may view as onerous much less intimidating, and will serve the organization well in the long haul.

STARTING FROM SCRATCH

Most organizations have some type of policy or procedure for annual staff assessment already in place, even though they may not be diligently followed or completed on a regular or routine basis. Sometimes, though, new directors or managers find themselves in the positon of having to introduce or create a new system for performance evaluation. If this is the case, introduce the process incrementally, allow the staff time for input, and allow time to adapt and fine-tune the process.

A good place to start is to ask peers from other libraries and organizations with similar missions to share the tools they use. So, for example, if you are in a corporate or special library setting, seek out colleagues in similar organizations. Often they will be able to provide a generic template that then can be adapted to your setting. Ask more seasoned managers, supervisors, and human resources staff about approaches they have tried, and what may or may not have worked. If you have access to the person whom you are replacing, ask them about the process. Management texts such as *Library and Information Center Management* (Moran, Stueart, and Morner 2013) can provide salient guidance as well.

There are numerous and varied approaches to conducting performance reviews and providing feedback, such as peer review, used in academic and research settings, upward reviews where subordinates assess their direct supervisors, and the 360-degree approach where feedback from many individuals (e.g., peers, managers, direct reports, external customers) is used to inform the process (Beehr, Ivanitskaya, Hansen, Erofeev, and Gudanowski 2001; Davidson 2007). In many settings, the direct supervisor still performs the performance review.

PEER REVIEW PROCESS IN A SPECIAL LIBRARY SETTING

At one time, I was hired to create a health services research library for a think tank within a health insurance company. In an organization with thousands of employees, I was the only librarian. I provided support to a small team of epidemiologists and researchers who were conducting original research in the health outcomes field. When it came time for evaluations, each member of the department was asked to provide input for my feedback. This meant that in addition to the six to eight researchers whom I supported, administrative and research assistants, data analysts, and other support staff also commented on my performance. While their reports were always positive, most of these individuals had very little interaction with me or access to data with which to evaluate how I was performing my duties. The process was more akin to a popularity contest than an opportunity for constructive feedback. In addition, the evaluations were not staggered in terms of timing, and so everyone was providing input for many colleagues at the same time. This meant the first requests for input received the highest number of responses. The folks who were at the end of the list, even though they may have had stellar performances, were likely to receive much less feedback from their colleagues, due to "input fatigue." While the aim of the process was based on the 360-degree model and was meant to be inclusive, in practice, the feedback provided was anemic and did not serve to inform or improve performance among the majority of staff members.

In this chapter, the focus is on an objectives-based performance review process, one that

- Allows for interaction and staff input
- Engages staff throughout the process
- Can be instituted with varying levels of positions
- Can be adapted to various management settings

The objectives-based approach to performance reviews makes expectations clear, performance measurable, and helps to match staff goals with institutional goals.

SECURING STAFF BUY-IN

As with any organizational process that has a direct impact upon operational procedures, involving staff in the process from the start will help to ensure cooperation, if not enthusiasm. For the new manager, this can be introduced as a way for staff to discuss expectations of their supervision and what areas might require the manager's support. Start by dedicating a staff meeting or even a half-day retreat, if possible, to brainstorm about what an ideal process for receiving feedback would look like. If the library has a mission or vision statement, the review process can be framed as the staff's road map to move from where the library is to where the library should be according to the mission, and ideally, how the staff performance can lend to that process. Allow staff to have input on what form the feedback should take (e.g., written feedback with dedicated meetings with the supervisor) and how often (e.g., comprehensive annual assessment, with midterm meeting).

Ask for concrete examples of information they would like to have included in their performance assessments. Plan ahead, and have ready best-case and worst-case examples of other organizations' forms to get the conversation going. If they are willing, ask staff members to share their own examples from previous experience, and what they found helpful or unproductive in the feedback process. Moreover, make an inventory of what assets you have within the library to support and develop staff (e.g., tuition sharing, flextime possibilities, and funds and board support to support workshop attendance). There is little value in assessing staff's professional development goals if you cannot offer some support for them (see chapter 5 for a discussion of staff development opportunities).

Using Goals and Objectives to Determine Expectations and Tasks

A logical place to start for determining and constructing goals and objectives of specific staff positions is the job description. A well-defined job description that allows some flexibility can provide context while streamlining the process at the same time (see chapter 2 for more guidance on creating job descriptions). Key responsibilities can guide overarching goals or expectations that then help determine specific, measurable objectives that are accomplished via tasks. Table 6.1 gives an example of the position of adult services librarian where a key responsibility is providing programs that are responsive to community needs.

Ideally, key responsibilities will be spelled out clearly in the job description for each position. If such a job description does not exist, working with the staff member to create their work description can be a constructive and useful exercise. Early on in their tenure, staff should meet with their direct supervisor to review their key responsibilities and to discuss and agree upon

Table 6.1.   Using Goals and Objectives to Guide Expectations and Tasks

Key Responsibility	Goal	Expectations	Objectives	Tasks
Determine and provide responsive adult programming for community that library serves.	Variety of well-attended programs; positive feedback from attendees.	Determine community needs and interests; provide programs that address those interests.	Community participation rate of X%; number of different programs (according to community preferences).	Complete community-wide survey with X% response rate within specified time period; use results to guide programming; provide X number of programs.

expectations and tasks for fulfilling those responsibilities, and how they will be measured. Figure 6.1 depicts the interactive nature of how goals and objectives relate to staff feedback and performance. Regular feedback ensures that staff members are not operating in a vacuum and their understanding of the

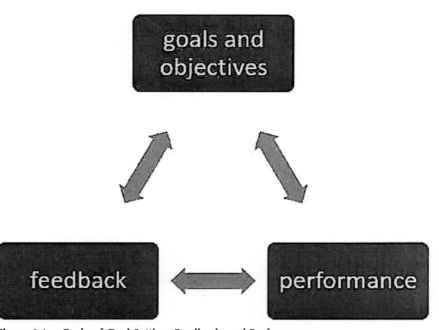

Figure 6.1.   Cycle of Goal Setting, Feedback, and Performance

goals and objectives that guide their duties are in keeping with organizational expectations.

A well-designed template can aid immensely in the process of performance reviews. See the following text box for a description of implementing the process from scratch in a small public library. For an example of the appraisal form used in that case, which can be adapted for most settings and to many different staff positions (i.e., circulation, reference, management, etc.), please refer to the text box in the section that follows this one.

ESTABLISHING THE REVIEW PROCESS AT A SMALL PUBLIC LIBRARY

Some years ago, when I started my position as the director of a small, rural public library, I replaced a director who was retiring after twenty-eight years of service. We overlapped a bit, and she graciously showed me the ropes and imparted a lot of helpful information that eased the transition tremendously. She had seen the library through many changes, including capital improvements that doubled the size of the facility, and had engendered tremendous support for the library in the community. When I asked if there was anything in particular I needed to know in terms of personnel, she provided a list of the staff and their corresponding "collectibles." For instance, Anita liked polar bears, Jane liked butterflies, and Paula liked hedgehogs. She said this information was important when it came to birthday and Christmas gifts for the staff. I combed through file drawers looking for records of previous reviews or details on staff job descriptions, or any personnel documentation whatsoever, but found nothing. So I asked the former director where I might find these types of files, and she responded, "Oh, I keep those in my trunk." I tried not to sputter and said, "In your car trunk?" She responded affirmatively, adding, "I don't like the message a locked cabinet sends to the staff; they might think I don't trust them." We met in the parking lot, where I retrieved the stack of files, hoping for a better understanding of the staff's positions within the library structure.

Once I retrieved the records, I found some of the staff members had completed cursory self-assessments where they described some of their job duties and how they felt about performing them. These were two to three years old, and had not been updated since. They didn't include any goals, objectives, or even clear delineation of job duties related to staff positions. Once I had settled into the director's position, a top priority was to develop a process for regular and ongoing feedback to the staff.

First, in order to understand what each position entailed, I proposed "shadowing" staff members for a day at a time to have a better grasp of specific job duties. With some staff this was quite welcomed and the process went smoothly, but for others it was such a departure from the previous director's style and approach, it was met with skepticism, and even fear. For those reluctant individuals, we had shorter meetings (an hour on average) in their workspace, where I asked them to walk me through their duties on a typical day. During this initial phase of my tenure, I also took each staff member out to lunch and "interviewed" them about their position, asking about changes they'd like to make, and what an ideal workday would include. This approach proved to be very beneficial in terms of establishing a congenial rapport and smoothing the way toward the next step in implementing an annual process for reviews.

Because there was not an established routine or template for performance reviews, I asked other directors in the local library consortium to share their process and any forms they used. Most did not have a formal process, and in many cases the staff positions were not comparable, so adapting the forms was a bit cumbersome. I then reached out to colleagues in nonprofit organizations and found a form I could adapt for use in the library, which is included here in the text box that follows. As an integral part of the new system, we also installed filing cabinets in the director's office that could be locked. Converse to the previous director's assumptions, staff were happy that their records were secure, and after time they embraced the regular process for feedback that was created.

CONDUCTING PERFORMANCE APPRAISALS

Even though it may be difficult to squeeze into a busy schedule, it is vitally important to dedicate and set aside adequate time to conduct thorough performance reviews. In this way, staff members receive the message that they are valued and valuable team members. A comfortable atmosphere should be cultivated, where the staff member is encouraged to engage in productive give-and-take with their supervisor. Managers have to assess for themselves how this environment is best created. It may include offering a cup of tea or a glass of water, sitting in a private, comfortable place, or moving to a quiet place; these efforts can help to create an environment that communicates the manager is keen to listen. Be sure to convey that a major part of this encounter is for the manager to be engaged, and to listen and learn. The two fundamental goals are for the supervisor to learn new aspects of possible shortcomings and unmet support needs regarding the supervisee, and for the supervisee to learn what they can do even better and how the library or organization can help them to get there. These are hard to achieve in distracting or threatening settings; the preferred environment should allow for a one-on-one encounter, optimally with no allowance for interruptions.

As described in the performance review sample form, an initial meeting should take place at the time of hire to review key responsibilities and then agree upon performance measurement parameters. In other words, what are the duties of the position, including expectations and related tasks? At the midterm point, or approximately six months after hiring, another meeting should take place to revisit and discuss these job components in order to make any necessary changes. If there are changes, these should be mutually agreed upon by the staff member and supervisor and recorded in an updated performance review form.

SAMPLE: PERFORMANCE REVIEW FORM

The review cycle may vary based upon first meeting and date of hire, but the standard cycle is

- ***Time of hire***—*supervisor completes the first two columns of Section One, key responsibilities and tasks are defined, other areas of the form are reviewed and discussed to clarify expectations, supervisor and staff member agree on method of communication regarding progress on expectations;*
- ***Six months (midpoint of annual process)***—*interim review, responsibilities and expectations are reviewed and adjusted as needed, method of communicating regarding progress of expectations is reconfirmed;*
- ***One year (annual review)***—*supervisor completes the performance review capturing the staff member's contributions to the department and the organization for the year. Expectations for the coming year are set and the cycle begins again.*

Employee's Name: _____

Position/Title: _____

Department: _____

Date Appointed to Current Position: ___/___/___ **Date Review Was Completed:** ___/___/___

Review Covers the Performance Period: ___/___/___ **to:** ___/___/___

Reviewer's Name: _____

Position/Title: _____

1. Key Responsibilities

The staff member and supervisor should determine the key responsibilities up to a maximum of seven. Responsibilities, and the means of measuring them, are defined at the start of the review cycle in January (or at the time of hire). They may need to be revised as tasks and responsibilities change (review midyear). The third column, "Accomplished Tasks," should be completed at the end of the review cycle in December.

January	*July*	*December*
	(Reviewed at midpoint)	

2. Key Performance Categories

The ratings in this section should be discussed in January (or time of hire) and July (at six months posthire) but completed at the end of the review period (December). The prereview discussions should clarify for the employee and supervisor performance factors and ratings in the context of key responsibilities.

Key Responsibilities	Measured by These Expectations and Tasks	Accomplished Tasks

Ratings: E = Exceptional, **C** = Commendable, **S** = Satisfactory, **U** = Unsatisfactory

Teamwork Skills	E	C	S	U
• Works well with other staff members.				
• Solicits input from other departments on issues of mutual interest.				
• Communicates policies/procedures to other departments effectively.				
• Works to create solutions to problems when collaborating with staff.				
Quality of Work	E	C	S	U
• Consistently meets deadlines in a thorough and accurate manner.				
• Organizes and plans work and is able to deal with unexpected demands.				
• Identifies, analyzes, and innovatively solves problems.				
• Performs work independently, involving supervisor when necessary.				
• Punctual—starts work on time, attends meetings in a timely fashion.				

• Final results require minimum checking and correction.				
• Seeks new and more efficient means for performing job (where appropriate).				

Quantity of Work	E	C	S	U
• Volume meets expectations relative to position requirements.				
• Utilizes resources (time, dollars) efficiently in producing work.				

Organization of Work	E	C	S	U
• Manages time effectively.				
• Takes initiative, finds innovative ways to get the job done within budget.				
• Plans, schedules, and monitors progress of work.				
• Prioritizes assignments and duties.				
• Produces yearly strategic plan (where appropriate).				
• Demonstrates resourcefulness and self-reliance.				

Job Knowledge and Technical Skills	E	C	S	U
• Utilizes necessary knowledge and skills to perform job.				
• Stays current, understands relevant job changes and developments.				
• Actively strives to keep current with new technology in area of responsibility.				
Quickly understands and applies knowledge.				

Communication Skills	E	C	S	U
• Listens effectively, demonstrates understanding of information received.				
• Writes clearly and convincingly.				
• Speaks clearly, logically, and convincingly.				
• Presents a positive image of the library when communicating with others.				

Supervision and Management (for staff with these duties)	E	C	S	U
• Effectively prepares budgets and maintains them.				
• Provides regular and candid feedback, including timely and thorough reviews.				
• Delegates responsibilities and tasks to maximize resource use.				
• Develops staff through coaching and training.				
• Seeks creative means to maximize talents of every direct report.				

3. Overall Job Performance

The space below is for the supervisor's comments on staff performance. Be sure to address accomplishments and areas that need improvement or special circumstances that may have affected job performance. Avoid ambiguous references. Quoting employee remarks and the use of examples will provide clarity and add value to the recording of a staff member's contributions.

1. Strengths, accomplishments

2. Opportunities for improvement

3. General comments, recommendations

4. Career Development

1. List the areas the staff member can focus on for further professional development.
2. What training classes or other opportunities would be helpful to the staff member?

5. Self-Evaluation

To be completed by staff member. Set aside space here so that a staff member can, if they wish, reflect upon the past year, capture their accomplishments, challenges, and provide comments.

It is recommended that the staff member complete this section prior to the December review meeting in preparation to discuss the year's progress.

6. Overall Rating

- **Exceptional**—Performance exceeds all expectations.
- **Commendable**—Performance exceeds many of the expectations of the job description.
- **Satisfactory**—Performance meets the expectations of the job description.
- **Unsatisfactory**—Performance does not meet job requirements and needs close supervision.

If performance has not improved within a specified period, the supervisor in consultation with the appropriate staff (e.g., director, human resources department) and in accordance with policies, may terminate employment.

Description of Ratings

Exceptional: Staff member has not only effectively met all discussed expectations within or before set deadlines, but has also managed unanticipated, complex projects within deadlines. Further, the staff member has contributed to creatively solving library and departmental challenges.

Commendable: Staff member consistently meets set expectations and time frames as well as successfully completing additional projects assigned as needed. Makes positive contributions to library and departmental challenges.

Satisfactory: Staff member is right on target in meeting their expectations within specified time frames. Provides positive comments/suggestions to library and departmental challenges.

Unsatisfactory: Staff member is not able to meet expectations and time frames. Requires immediate discussion with supervisor to correct situation. This warning may not constitute termination; however, depending on the circumstances, it can result in termination. This requires consultation with the departmental supervisor.

7. Observations on the Review Process

This section gives the staff member an opportunity to comment on the process. A section is set aside for general comments, should a staff member wish to bring up additional items.

Performance Planning
Developed staff member's key responsibilities and tasks including the appropriate measures of success. Conducted performance review on time.

Ongoing Feedback
Provides timely and constructive feedback in an effective manner. Demonstrates a clear understanding of pressures and demands of the work environment.

Interim Review
Conducted interim review on time. Solicited staff member's comments and feedback during review meeting. (Supervisors are expected to conduct an interim review meeting at midyear to discuss accomplishments and suggest areas of improvement.)

Signed by:
Staff Member _____Date __/__/__
Supervisor (Reviewer) _____Date __/__/__

Informal Feedback

Of course, feedback that happens outside of formally scheduled intervals is happening all the time. This can be as simple as verbally recognizing a task well done. The old rule of thumb "praise in public, criticize in private" should be followed when dispensing informal feedback. Try not to shy away from constructive criticism; in instances where you are required to give difficult feedback, remember to describe how positive change can be implemented and give clear instructions for expectations. Allow time and space for staff members to respond. Take advantage of opportunities for team building where you can. For instance, for the midterm meeting that occurs halfway through the annual review cycle, a less formal coffee or lunchtime gathering can engender a collaborative and positive atmosphere.

Tips for Streamlining the Process

- Keep good records.
  - Make notes throughout the year (e.g., in a specified computer file, bound notebook).
    - They don't have to be extensive; ensure they jog your memory and record the event.
    - Ask staff for documentation of continuing education and training they have completed over the year and include it in their file.
    - Include positive and negative occurrences of events.
    - Include feedback received from external parties (other staff, patrons, etc.).
      - Use different font colors for easy categorization and location.
      - Concrete examples with dates and descriptions are very effective for sharing with staff during performance review meetings.
      - Direct quotes can be informative, evocative, and powerful reminders.
- Act upon results of performance review meetings
  - Send staff to workshops and conferences.
  - Arrange for in-house training for skill development.
  - Follow up on any issues or concerns that arise.
- Allow staff to think out of the box.
  - Ask where they'd like to be in three to five years' time, "in an ideal world."
  - Consider their input carefully.
  - Encourage self-assessment and allow time for reflection.
- Remember sometimes there are issues outside of a staff member's control.
  - Scheduling difficulties
  - Dependency upon another department or external force
  - Life events

There are a number of contributory components in the feedback process, as described in figure 6.2. The job description is the framework that helps determine goals and objectives, and performance expectations. With agreed-upon performance measurement and consideration of whether tasks and duties have been completed successfully, the feedback process can be completed in an objective manner.

INSTITUTIONALIZING THE PROCESS

Once you have created a protocol or process for engaged feedback, regularize it by scheduling it for the same time of the year. Look at the organizational

Figure 6.2.   Components of the Feedback Process

calendar and strive to schedule the performance reviews when there are not likely to be competing interests, such as budget preparations, summer reading programs, new student orientation, and so on. Examine the organizational chart and see where it makes sense to delegate (e.g., the assistant director can handle branch employees, the administrative assistant can oversee the part-time circulation clerks, etc.).

The annual review process can aid in identifying "big picture" issues in the organization, such as policy absence or shortcomings. For example, there was the case in a public library where the children's program coordinator, on occasion, brought her teenage daughter to the library to assist with summer program activities. Although this was somewhat informal, the teenager did act as a volunteer and completed the volunteer training process.

When a new assistant director was hired, she also started bringing her children to work: her daughter, also a teenager, and her ten-year-old son. As she lived sixty miles away, there were times when her children were at the library with her for the entire day. This usually occurred when the director was at all-day meetings or working away from the library. During the interim review meetings, other staff members reported the disruption caused by the assistant director's son, and so the director approached her to discuss the issue. The assistant director immediately became defensive and referred to the precedence of the children's program coordinator's daughter as a volunteer. It became apparent there were no policies or procedural guidelines for addressing the issue of bringing children to work, or the minimum age of volunteers. The fact that the review meetings allowed for the opportunity of private discussion resulted in an impromptu policy analysis. As a result, the policy committee of the library board was consulted. A new policy was crafted and approved, resulting in guidelines to ensure fair treatment across the organization.

Another area where the review process can be particularly informative is in identifying training needs. When given a regular, formalized opportunity for self-assessment and reflection, often staff will make their wishes known when it comes to skill development and areas where they would benefit from training. As it can be difficult to anticipate training needs for a wide variety of positions and levels of staff, allowing self-identification of needs is a win-win situation for an engaged supervisor. In addition, data gathered during staff reviews can be brought to administrators to justify continuing education and funding to promote staff's continuous learning and skill development.

It is unavoidable that some reviews will contain unfavorable and possibly contested critiques. Thus, it is important that the use of the review (e.g., as a tool for formalizing the communication of expectations between supervisors and staff, as a record for assessing staff progress, for prioritizing pay increases, etc.) is made clear to staff members. For serious disagreements in assessment, a policy with a process for appeal should be established in writing (e.g., assistant director assessments can be discussed with the director upon request, but the board will not discuss reviews with an employee, unless it is in writing and part of a termination action). The following text box provides an example of a simple form for the appeals process that can be adapted to most library settings.

SAMPLE: PERFORMANCE REVIEW APPEAL FORM

When an employee believes the overall rating or individual performance factor ratings do not represent a true evaluation of their work performance during the appraisal period, they may file an appeal. Such an appeal will follow the normal organizational ladder. Within ten days of receipt of the signed performance appraisal form (after the annual performance review meeting), the employee should meet with their supervisor in an attempt to resolve the disagreement before filing a formal appeal. The employee is encouraged to complete and use the Performance Review Appeal Form as the basis of initial discussion with their supervisor. If not resolved in the informal discussion with the supervisor, the employee may formally appeal the evaluation by completing and submitting this Performance Review Appeal Form to the evaluating supervisor. If the appeal is not resolved by the immediate supervisor, it is the appellant's responsibility to move the appeal through the subsequent steps in a timely manner.

Name:_____ Date: _____

Title: _____Supervisor Name: _____

Date of Review: _____ Date Signed Copy Received: _____

1. Please identify the performance categories you are contesting (for example, teamwork skills, quality, quantity and/or organization of work, communication skills, etc.).

2. Please identify the supervisor's rating for each of the categories you are appealing, and the rating you would propose for each of the categories.

3. Please provide the specific facts (with examples and any evidence) to support your appeal for each category rating.

NOTE: A complete copy of the Performance Review Form you are appealing (signed by the evaluating supervisor) must be submitted with this appeal at each step of the appeal process.

Signature of Appellant: _____Date Submitted: _____

Signature of Supervisor: _____Date Received: _____

The next section includes the decision and signature boxes for immediate supervisor, department manager, and department director (if needed).

Employee Name: _____

Immediate Supervisor
• The following solution was reached:

The revised performance feedback appraisal form is attached.

• We have not resolved this appeal; the employee may carry appeal forward to next level of management.

Signature of Appellant: _____ Date: _____
Signature of Supervisor: _____ Date: _____

Department Manager/Next Level of Management above Supervisor
Date appeal was received: _____

• The following solution was reached:

The revised performance feedback appraisal form is attached.

• We have not resolved this appeal; the employee may carry appeal forward to next level of management.

Signature of Appellant: _____ Date: _____
Signature of Supervisor: _____ Date: _____

Department Director
Date appeal was received: _____

• The following solution was reached:

The revised performance feedback appraisal form is attached.

• We have not resolved this appeal; the employee may carry appeal forward to next level of management.

Signature of Appellant: _____ Date: _____
Signature of Supervisor: _____ Date: _____

Attach additional sheets as necessary.

On those occasions, hopefully rare, when staff take exception to some aspect of their evaluation, they will likely be emotional and not long-term oriented. Thus, having the appeal process previously clarified will prevent them from feeling the process is treating them uniquely or unfairly. Provide a clear description of the process in the employee handbook, make sure each new employee goes through the process of setting goals, objectives, and so on shortly after their initial orientation and during their first one to three months. Over time, staff members will come to expect regular, ongoing feedback and may even evolve to look forward to and welcome it.

Tips for Handling an Appeal

- Allow the employee adequate time and opportunity to discuss concerns.
- Keep channels of communication open.
- Keep the conversation focused on elements of the dispute.
- Examine how similar cases were handled in the past.
- Have evidence ready to justify the review.
- Identify the resolution the employee is seeking.
- Keep clear records of process and decisions.
- Adhere to time frame for the appeal procedure.
- Use the appeal process as a necessary management tool.

IN CLOSING

In busy organizations, regularly scheduled feedback may be overlooked, and with engaged and high-performing staff members, the need for performance reviews may not be obvious. Clear, objective-driven feedback with agreed-upon goals and performance measures can help to ensure staff feel valued and receive the guidance and support they need for ongoing stellar performance.

BIBLIOGRAPHY

Beehr, Terry A., Lana Ivanitskaya, Curtiss P. Hansen, Dmitry Erofeev, and David M. Gudanowski. 2001. "Evaluation of 360 Degree Feedback Ratings: Relationships with Each Other and with Performance and Selection Predictors." *Journal of Organizational Behavior* 22: 775–788.
Davidson, Melissa L. 2007. "The 360 Evaluation." *Clinics in Podiatric Medicine and Surgery* 24 (1): 65–94.
Moran, B., R. Stueart, and C. Morner. 2013. *Library and Information Center Management.* Santa Barbara, CA: Libraries Unlimited.

"Top 76 Quotes on Performance Management." Cognology, accessed July 7, 2016, http://www.cognology.com.au/75-performance-quotes/.

"Top Ten Quotes on Evaluation." OwlRe Wise Research and Evaluation, accessed July 7, 2016, http://www.owlre.com/wordpress/wp-content/uploads/2008/01/fact-sheet_owlre_quotes.pdf.

Chapter Seven

Additional Funding Sources for Staffing Activities

"Only in our dreams are we free. The rest of the time we need wages."

—Terry Pratchett

"A budget tells us what we can't afford, but it doesn't keep us from buying it."

—William Feather

As budgets become tighter in all types of libraries, alternative funding sources can be an important resource for supplementing regular funding and extending services. Depending on the agency and opportunities, supplemental funds can be used for a wide spectrum of activities, from capital initiatives to specialized programs and technology provision to creating and supporting staff development activities. While fund-raising encompasses a broad spectrum of activities, this chapter will be focused more specifically on identifying opportunities related to supplying, supporting, and supplementing staff development activities.

GRANTS, SCHOLARSHIPS, AND FELLOWSHIPS

Grants, scholarships, and fellowships are common mechanisms for funding staff development activities. While the application process may seem daunting at first, grant writing is a skill that can be developed through practice and persistence. The best advice for getting grants is to identify the appropriate opportunity, follow the instructions thoroughly, and apply. Remember too, competition for funds can be keen, so if at first you don't succeed, do try again. Some of the ways grants can provide support for staffing and staff development include

- Hiring
- Continuing education
  - Training
  - Scholarships
  - Conference attendance
    - Workshops, preconference education
    - Travel
- Research support
- Enabling specialized program provision
- Staff recognition and awards

Encourage staff on all levels to be on the lookout for opportunities and allow support for applying for funding. That support can range from aid with composing and compiling the actual applications to encouraging attendance in grant-writing workshops to having dedicated grant writers and development officers on staff.

Federal and State Agencies

There are a number of federal agencies involved in supporting library activities and initiatives. The logical starting place for searching for grants from federal agencies is www.grants.gov. The site includes a grant learning center to get started, links to grant-making agencies, information for applicants, and options for searching the grant database, such as by organization type or by using keywords.

Another way is to start directly with the agencies that support libraries. The primary agency for library support is the Institute of Museum and Library Services (IMLS, www.imls.gov). The IMLS has a variety of programs that support staff, such as National Leadership Grants, the National Medal for Museum and Library Service, and the Laura Bush 21st Century Librarian Program. The IMLS also provides grants to states through State Library Administrative Agencies (SLAAs), which are used to support statewide services and initiatives through cooperative agreements or subgrant competitions from public, school, special, research, and academic libraries (www.imls.gov/grants/grants-states).

Other federal agencies that support educational and library activities include the National Archives and Records Administration (www.archives.

gov), which supports professional education for archivists; the National Endowment for the Arts (www.nea.gov), which supports opportunities for arts participation; the National Endowment for the Humanities (www.neh. gov), which has a variety of programs related to institutional support for libraries and museums; and the Department of Health and Human Services (www.hhs.gov), through the National Institutes of Health (NIH, www.nih. gov), which includes the National Library of Medicine (www.nlm.nih.gov). While the NIH is focused specifically on health research, they also support research-related activities, such as funding for training and fellowships (e.g., the NLM Library Associate Fellowship Program; www.nlm.nih.gov/ about/training/associate/), career development, resources, and scientific conferences.

Another resource for funds and opportunities can be through state agencies. As mentioned above, the IMLS disburses funding to libraries through the State Library Administrative Agencies. According to the IMLS (2014), the SLAAs in all fifty states and the District of Columbia provided services to public libraries in the form of consulting services, continuing education programs, summer reading program support, and service program review. They provided continuing education programs to academic libraries in forty states, to school library media centers in forty-one states, and to special libraries in forty-two states. SLAAs are an important venue for training and educational opportunities for libraries of all types nationwide. State library organizations or associations are another funding venue, especially for staff awards for conference participation, travel, and recognition.

Tips on Grant Writing

- Start with a good idea.
- Identify appropriate funder and program.
- Prepare early and allow enough time for a strong application.
- Follow directions thoroughly.
- Be concise and specific in language.
- Articulate enthusiasm for the project.
- Use examples when appropriate.
- Be focused.
- Edit meticulously.
- Solicit feedback from a trusted colleague or mentor.
- Have contingencies for unexpected circumstances.
- Attend carefully to deadlines.

BE CAREFUL WHAT YOU WISH FOR

When I started as a public library director after a long career in health science libraries, I was excited at the prospect of bridging the communities of practice and extending health information opportunities into the wider community. I started by visiting the administrators of the four hospitals located in our county (it should be noted this was a very rural, large geographical area, about the size of the state of Rhode Island), and asking about their health care staffs' information needs. All four agreed that they would welcome resources and training for their physicians and nurses on using and finding authoritative health information. I identified a health information system grant from the National Library of Medicine (NLM) and applied for funding to hire a medical librarian as an outreach coordinator and to provide for laptops for installation in the hospital staff lounges and patient waiting areas. The funding process was a slow one. We weren't successful in our first application, but we were encouraged to reapply. One of the concerns of the grant reviewers was that it might be difficult to find a medical librarian who wanted to work independently in a very rural part of New York State. This concern was addressed by proposing that if we had difficulty hiring, then I would complete the tasks. We advertised widely for a medical librarian. After I attended the annual Medical Library Association conference and met with candidates at the career center, we hired a newly graduated MLIS student to fill the post.

As often happens, the nature of the project changed. Between the time of applying for the grant and receiving it, two of the hospital administrators had left their institutions; the new administrators were no longer interested in the resources or training. Also, the hospital in the village where the library was located declared bankruptcy and closed. In the fourth setting, though, the project was very successful; the majority of health care staff were trained to use the NLM's resources effectively and received Continuing Medical Education (CME) credits for completion of training. Patients learned to use MedlinePlus to search for information while waiting for appointments.

Because of the failure to reach our intended audiences in the hospital settings, we expanded the project to provide training to health care staff in rural clinics and in neighboring public libraries. Halfway through the project, however, the medical librarian quit. It seems the frustration she experienced in adapting the project was too much for her, so as was stipulated in the application, I completed the project. What I gleaned from the endeavor was to be flexible and ready to adapt in order to achieve desired project outcomes, and that learning comes in unexpected ways. For a more detailed description of the project, please see Mary Grace Flaherty and Les Roberts, 2009, "Rural Outreach Training Efforts to Clinicians and Public Library Staff: NLM Resource Promotion," *Journal of Consumer Health on the Internet* 13 (1): 14–30.

Professional Organizations

Professional library associations are another venue for locating financial support for library staff development through grants, fellowships, scholarships, and stipends. Encourage your staff to become involved in the profession through active membership in the professional association that corresponds to their field. If you're involved in teaching new librarians, encourage your students to join the appropriate association at the reduced entry membership fee level for students. Listed below are some of the opportunities available through a selection of professional library associations. Many of the organizations offer support for conference attendance, especially for new members.

American Library Association

The American Library Association has an extensive listing of grants and awards listed on their website (ALA; www.ala.org/awardsgrants/). These range from leadership and research grants, such as the ABC-CLIO Leadership Grant for school library associations and the Diversity Research Grant to increase knowledge on diversity issues in the field, to conference and international travel grants, such as the EBSCO/ALA Annual Conference Sponsorship award and the Bogle Pratt International Travel Fund. There are some dedicated to professional development, such as the Pat Carterette Professional Development Grant, and some are fellowship grants for specific activities; for example, the Louise Seaman Bechtel Fellowship. The ALA's Spectrum Scholarship program offers opportunities for individuals from underrepresented communities. The ALA also offers many awards for professional recognition. For the complete listing, see www.ala.org/awardsgrants/awards/browse/prec?showfilter=no.

Divisions and sections of the ALA, such as the Association of College and Research Libraries, the largest division of the ALA and arm for academic and research librarians, also offer opportunities (www.ala.org/acrl/awards), including student and early career scholarships and the Barbara-Bonous-Smit

scholarship for academic librarians with under five years' post-MLIS experience. The division for public libraries, the Public Library Association, also
has a number of awards and grants (www.ala.org/pla/awards), ranging from
recognition for innovative service (Upstart Innovation Award), knowledge
(the Allie Beth Martin Award), risk taking (the Charlie Robinson Award),
protection of intellectual freedom (the Gordon M. Conable Award), and leadership (the Demco New Leaders Travel Grant), to mention a few.

Another helpful resource is *The ALA Book of Library Grant Money*, now in
its ninth edition in 2014. This comprehensive guide includes ways to become
"grant-ready" and has an exhaustive list of opportunities available from private and corporate foundations, direct corporate givers, government agencies,
and nonprofit and library organizations. In order to be included in the directory, the funder must have a history of making grants to libraries.

Association for Library and Information Science Education

The Association for Library and Information Science Education (ALISE;
www.alise.org/awards-grants) is a nonprofit organization geared toward
faculty, staff, and students in the library and information science profession.
They offer a number of opportunities for contribution to the profession and
general awards, such as the ALISE Service Award and the Award for Professional Contribution. Awards to attend the annual conference and research
competition awards, for example the ALISE/Connie Van Fleet for Research
Excellence in Public Library Service to Adults and the ALISE Research
Grant Competition, are also offered through this organization.

Medical Library Association

The Medical Library Association has a number of grants, scholarships, and
fellowships available for health sciences librarians at all stages in their careers (www.mlanet.org/p/cm/ld/fid=47). For those who are new to the field,
there are the Continuing Education Grant and the EBSCO/MLA Annual
Meeting Grant. The Hospital Libraries Section offers a professional development grant for hospital librarians and those who work in clinical settings;
the Medical Informatics section offers a career development grant as well.
The MLA/NLM Spectrum Scholarship, in conjunction with NLM, supports
two ALA Spectrum Scholars to aid minority individuals to obtain a graduate
degree and work in the field. MLA also has a scholarship program for students enrolled in or entering an ALA-accredited library program and one for
minority students as well.

For professionals at the midcareer level, the following opportunities are
available: for attendance at the MLA's annual conference, the Ysabel Ber-
tolucci MLA Annual Meeting Grant; for individuals working with Hispanic/

Latino community information services, there is the Naomi C. Broering Hispanic Heritage Grant; the Eugene Garfield Research Fellowship offers funding for research on the history of information sciences to enhance our practice; and the Donald A. B. Lindberg Research Fellowship supports research on linking library services to improved health care. The David A. Kronick Traveling Fellowship covers expenses for traveling for study of health information management.

The MLA also has some opportunities with an international focus: the Cunningham Memorial International Fellowship allows for international health sciences librarians to visit the United States or Canada; the Librarians without Borders® Ursula Poland International Scholarship allows for a Canadian or U.S. librarian to work on an international library project; and the MLA HINARI/Research4Life (R4L) Grant supports training in emerging and low-income countries.

Sections and chapters of the MLA also provide opportunities, which can be found at www.mlanet.org/page/mla-section-sponsored-awards-and-grants and www.mlanet.org/page/chapter-awards-and-honors respectively.

The MLA also has a grants coordinator on staff, who can be reached via e-mail at awards@mail.mlahq.org.

Other Organizations

Of course this list is not meant to be exhaustive, but to serve as a starting point. There are other national professional organizations for librarians that offer opportunities that are not included here, such as the Special Libraries Association (SLA), although according to their website as of November 2016, "Financial constraints may have put SLA research grants on hold, but not research itself" (www.sla.org/research-is-alive-and-well-in-sla/). The Association for Rural and Small Libraries (ARSL; www.arsl.info) is another example; they offer a scholarship to attend their annual conference.

As with ALA and MLA, sections and chapters of professional organizations are another valuable venue for locating funding for staff activities. As new opportunities arise and are created, it is important to keep informed through active membership.

READ AND REACH: A RESOURCE FOR PROMOTING PHYSICAL ACTIVITY IN CHILDREN'S STORYTIME PROGRAMS

There are opportunities for supporting staff development that at first blush may not be obvious. The ALA Carnegie-Whitney Grant (http://

www.ala.org/awardsgrants/carnegie-whitney-grant), a $5,000 award for the preparation of guides to library resources, was one of those instances for me. When I came across the announcement for the grant, I presented it as an example of different types of funding opportunities in the Management for Small Public Libraries class that I currently teach. Given my interest in health promotion in public libraries, I proposed the idea of a resource list for children's librarians that would promote physical activity, and then encouraged any students who might be interested in working on the project to meet with me. One of the students contacted me immediately, and we worked on the application together. The simple budget we submitted provided funding for the student to complete the project, travel funds for her to promote the resource through a panel presentation at the PLA biennial conference, and a small honorarium for children's book author and illustrator Suzanne Bloom to provide sketches for the web resource. The resource was completed (http:// readandreach.web.unc.edu/) and introduced to a lively crowd of approximately two hundred librarians at the PLA conference, just in time for the 2016 summer reading program theme of health and fitness. The student has since graduated and is now enjoying a successful start to her career as a teen librarian. Don't overlook what may seem like small funding opportunities; with minimal effort they can often provide big benefits where everyone wins.

Foundations

There are a number of foundations and funds that support library-related activities and initiatives. The Gates Foundation is well known for its historical support of technology provision and advocacy training for staff in U.S. public libraries. They have now shifted their priorities to global library efforts that support access to information (http://www.gatesfoundation.org/What-We-Do/Global-Development/Global-Libraries). The Elsevier Foundation supports research on improving health information in developing countries (www.elsevierfoundation.org). The John D. and Catherine T. MacArthur Foundation (www.macfound.org) offers funds for supporting educational initiatives. The Laura Bush Foundation (www.laurabushfoundation.com) provides funds to school libraries to update their collections and resources.

The above are just a few examples of the more widely known foundations that support library activities; a good starting point for locating foundation funding is the Foundation Center (www.foundationcenter.org). Their subscription-based online Foundation Directory includes a database of over

140,000 grant makers, with keyword and subject searching. Local foundations are another important resource for funding; get to know the foundations in your geographic region and what opportunities they might provide.

THE CONSUMER HEALTH INFORMATION CENTER, CRANDALL PUBLIC LIBRARY, GLENS FALLS, NEW YORK

In 1998, a local foundation advisor who was also a community member and library user approached the director of the Crandall Public Library with concern about the increasing amount of health information available via the Internet. She saw an opportunity to aid patrons in their search for reliable resources. The library director was already acquainted with the community member through their prior work together on Libraries for the Future, an advocacy program for libraries.

They agreed that creating a consumer health information center within the public library would be a viable way to attend to their community's health information needs. The director completed an application for funding, which included hiring a medical librarian to create and staff the center. The foundation funded the initial effort, and when it was successful, they renewed and increased the funding to keep the project going. The medical librarian worked closely with the hospital librarian in the town, creating a synergistic energy between the public library and the health care community. She successfully applied for funding through the National Library of Medicine to expand her efforts beyond the town and offered training on consumer health information regionally. The initial opportunity arose because the library director was well known and active in the larger community. The lesson here is to be visible, active, and connected so that you can be ready when opportunity knocks, in whatever form.

Other Resources

There are other community-based resources to consider as well. Service organizations, such as Rotary International, may offer scholarships and opportunities suitable for staff development. Private individuals and local businesses may offer funds for endowments or legacy gifts to support staff. Memorial funds, such as the Grace and Harold Sewell Memorial Fund (www.sewell-fund.org), offer opportunities such as learning partnerships for librarians to spend up to a year in a health care or research organization and stipends for attending national meetings. Friends of the Libraries Groups are another venue; in some public libraries the Friends Group sponsors staff training opportunities with funding and staff appreciation activities.

Keep a current "wish list" of staff opportunities, those things you would do or offer if a winning lottery ticket or wealthy benefactor came your way. Then when opportunity does knock, you'll be prepared.

Sustainability

An important and primary consideration for any type of external funding is how the grant-funded activity will be supported once the external funding has expired or funds have been exhausted. Some types of staff support, such as conference travel or professional recognition awards, won't require a plan; but grants that allow for hiring new staff or creating new initiatives will require sustainability planning. Consider carefully where future funding will come from (for instance, it may be that funds are shifted from other departments) and budget accordingly.

IN CLOSING

Fund-raising has been identified as a central component for the future and success of all types of libraries (Wood 2014). The opportunities provided through external funding for staff can be used for activities that improve and/or boost morale, from workshop and conference attendance to allowing for new services and programs. When it comes to searching out such opportunities, be creative and take chances. Remember, with external funding opportunities, if you don't make the effort to seek them out, you won't reap the benefits.

BIBLIOGRAPHY

Swan, D. W., J. Grimes, T. Owens, K. Miller, and L. Bauer. 2014. "State Library Administrative Agencies Survey: Fiscal Year 2012" (IMLS-2014-SLAA-01). Washington, D.C.: Institute of Museum and Library Services, accessed October 4, 2016, https://www.imls.gov/assets/1/AssetManager/2012%20SLAA%20Report.pdf.
"Wages Quotes." Brainy Quote, accessed October 4, 2016, http://www.brainyquote.com/quotes/keywords/wages.html.
Wood, M. Sandra. (ed.). 2014. *Successful Library Fundraising: Best Practices*. Lanham, MD: Rowman and Littlefield.

Chapter Eight

Going Forward

"When we strive to become better than we are, everything around us becomes better too."

—Paulo Coelho

"To live happily with other people one should ask of them only what they can give."

—Tristan Bernard

Rapidly changing technologies, combined with unprecedented access to all types of information, are causing myriad societal changes. As these changes are tied to the very heart and mission of libraries, organizationally, libraries are undergoing swift change. Shifts in expectations of what a library is, or can be, are resulting in new ways of service provision as well. As we respond to users and adapt to these changes, the need to keep skills current and to transform job duties is ever present and increasingly important. Given appropriate tools and a supportive environment, staff members can aid immensely during transitional times and contribute to organizational adaptability.

In this chapter, some of the factors that sustain organizational flexibility and well-being are discussed, such as open communication, team building, and workplace diversity. These are all constituent ingredients that help to create a proactive and adaptive organizational environment, in which staff are valued, encouraged, motivated, and can thrive.

COMMUNICATION

Open lines of communication are essential in instilling a sense of trust across organizations, and among and between staff members, at all organizational levels. In my experience, there is nothing more destructive to workplace productivity and tranquility, and overall staff well-being, than closed channels of communication. When communication is stifled, selective, or truncated, there can be resultant insecurity, secrecy, conjecture, gossip, formation of fractious factions, and high levels of distrust and dissatisfaction.

The practice of transparency in communication and action should start with organizational leadership. Sharing information not only conveys to employees that they are trusted, but has also been identified as one of the key practices of successful organizations (Pfeffer and Veiga 1999). In addition, it can help to instill staff ownership in the organization's success. If staff are aware of problems and any challenges the organization might be facing, they can be involved in identifying and enacting solutions. For example, in these times when libraries are increasingly expected to do more with less, staff may have valuable input on how resources should be allocated, eliminated, and/ or stretched. As frontline staff are constantly engaging with library users, they have an inside perspective on what services are used and what services are declining in popularity; solicit their candid input when making changes. Innovation increases when staff feel encouraged to express their ideas and opinions in a supportive atmosphere. Remember that individuals may receive and process information differently, so allow for differences in communication styles and preferences.

After almost twenty years of working in medical and health sciences libraries, I accepted a position as the director of a public library in a small, rural community. I was not from the area and was surprised when on my first day, one of the staff members asked candidly, "Why did you move here?" I was even more surprised when the staff member who ran the children's programs asked to meet with me concerning the summer reading program.

I started the position in early June, and summer reading was scheduled to kick off at the end of the month. It seems the rumors about my background and expectations had run rampant from the time of my interview in April until the time when I started in the position of director. The rumor that brought the children's program coordinator to my office on my second day was the wildest. She had "heard" that because

I didn't have any children of my own (which contributed to a general conclusion that I did not like kids), and because of my background in more "professional libraries" (e.g., academic and medical research), I was canceling all children's programs. Further, she was under the impression that there would be no summer reading activities after I started in the position of director. I could not have been more flabbergasted. There was absolutely no factual basis for this supposition, only speculation; in fact, I thought one of the most appealing factors of the public library environment would be the opportunity to engage with a more varied population of users. In other chapters in my life, I had been a nanny, a clown, a children's gymnastics instructor, a summer camp counselor, and had volunteered working with youths of all ages in all varieties of settings.

Once I recovered my composure, I assured her that this was indeed an unsubstantiated claim, and our children's programs would continue to enjoy the full support of the director. The encounter was an important early lesson for me in terms of misinformation and communication, and ended up setting the tone for my tenure at the library. We started every staff meeting with the opportunity for any staff member to voice their concerns or clarify something they had "heard." I also regularly reported on the monthly library board meetings so that all staff members were kept in the loop; we discussed any actions taken, pending issues, and so on. As much as possible, shifts on the circulation desk were rotated so that staff members interacted with a variety of colleagues. When appropriate, during the hiring process, I asked interviewees how they would deal with gossip in the workplace. Lastly, if I caught wind of the rumor mill churning up, I halted it by stepping in as soon as possible with open and clear communication.

When leaders communicate effectively, there are greater levels of satisfaction among staff (Madlock 2008). To ensure everyone in the organization is committed to open communication, managers should lead by example. Inasmuch as they can, managers should convey to their team on a regular basis, through formal and informal mechanisms, the actions they are taking and the rationale behind their actions. At all levels, managers should encourage two-way communication across the organization, which includes active listening and soliciting input. There should be a mechanism for employee grievances in place, and staff should be assured that any concerns or complaints they have will be kept confidential, if that is their preference. At the end of the day, libraries are all about providing access to information; this should apply to the internal function of the organization as well.

On the organizational level, the library should have a communication plan. These are commonly used in project management to keep stakeholders apprised. Communication plans allow for targeted communication and provide structure; they can also increase efficiency and effectiveness of external communication and make the process of ongoing communication easier in the long run. Elements of the communication plan include determining objectives (e.g., is there a direct purpose, such as communicating budget information or increasing awareness of services?), determining the audience (e.g., do you want to reach potential and/or new users?), and determining communication venues or channels (e.g., social media, website, local newspaper, etc.). The Pell Institute and Pathways to College Network have created a straightforward guide to help start the process: *Developing a Communication Plan.*

Regular assessment to ensure resources are serving the organizational mission should also be part of the library's ongoing activities. These assessments can help to identify areas where staff development is needed, and where changes might be needed. For example, user data and surveys may indicate a need for new services, with additional training needs for staff. When new initiatives are undertaken, devise ways to evaluate them and to measure their success and/or failure, and to communicate that with stakeholders.

Determine what spells success to your organization, and then create methods to measure. Is it numbers of attendees at programs, numbers of times a material has been checked out, numbers of likes on social media? Or maybe it's literacy levels, school attendance, and graduation rates. Increasingly, libraries of all types are in the position of justifying the need for their services, and in some cases their very existence. This pressure is accompanied by the need for accountability to our user communities, the capability to measure our value, and ways to communicate that value.

There are many ways to communicate information and reports to the public. One public library director came up with a very creative way to make the library's annual report reach a broader segment of her community. She engaged a local children's book illustrator to create a lively montage, highlighting the required statistics. She then had them printed and distributed to all of the major restaurants in the area, where they were used as placemats. They were produced in black and white, so they could also be used as coloring templates for local children as they dined. Anecdotal data showed that door counts increased after the campaign, and numbers of library cards for new users increased as well.

TEAM BUILDING

Team building is used to describe a wide variety of activities that are designed to create opportunities to increase collaboration among staff members in order to build trust, minimize conflict, and express appreciation. Activities are meant to allow staff to connect and interact in new and meaningful ways. In some instances, team building is used to address conflict or systemic communication problems; in effect, this is equivalent to closing the barn door after the horse has left. Team building can be utilized proactively to nurture and involve staff so that systemic issues are less likely to arise.

Some organizations have full-blown retreats for staff, or daylong outings off-site with specified objectives and outcomes that might involve rope courses, physical activities, rigorous agendas, and so on. Team-building activities don't have to be fancy or expensive, however. Something as simple as using icebreakers to start off a staff meeting (e.g., have each staff member tell a story about their name) or supplying access to fitness videos and equipment in the staff lounge that can allow for a quick pick-me-up might encourage spontaneous interaction and subsequent team building.

Allowing for and encouraging interdepartmental work projects can create new work groups and promote team building across the organization. There are many free and readily available online resources for getting started with team building. Challenge staff to form pairs or groups, then generate ideas and come up with innovative suggestions for activities and tasks that engender cooperation; then take turns leading activities.

Observing anniversaries and special events can be great opportunities for team building. When our circulation desk manager was celebrating her thirty-fifth anniversary at the public library, we asked how she would like to mark the occasion. She promptly responded, "I'd like to have a bowling party." We chose a Friday night (since the library closed at 6 p.m. on Fridays) at a local bowling lane, and attendance was voluntary. The Friends of the Library group sponsored the event, and every staff member was there to celebrate. Some were seasoned bowlers, and some had never picked up a bowling ball, but everyone had a great time. Teams were rotated, so everyone had a chance to interact with everyone else. There were fond, shared memories after the event that, when recalled, brought all the staff closer together. In fact, some of the staff formed a league team as a result of the happy celebration that continued for years thereafter.

Collaboration is an important ingredient in team building and should extend beyond a specific department or the library organization. Beyond mixing up work teams and duties, seek out opportunities for staff to interact with other constituent groups, whether it is business organizations, university departments, schools, or nonprofits. No matter the organizational setting, encourage library staff representation on committees and within the greater community. For example, staff who are involved in budget preparation and planning should get to know development officers. Staff members who are involved in solving space issues might become involved in community planning. In the public library setting, allow for training of staff to become literacy volunteers and encourage involvement in outreach programs with all types of local organizations.

DIVERSITY IN THE WORKPLACE

An analysis of *Fortune*'s "100 Best Companies to Work For" found that what distinguished superior workplaces were more staff development programs, diversity initiatives, and more fun work environments (Joyce 2003). In the work context, diversity is not limited to demographic differences (e.g., race, gender, age) but also includes differences in abilities, education, experience, and tenure at the organization. We have known for some time that heterogeneous groups, those that include a larger number of backgrounds and subsequent perspectives, can reach better solutions to problems (Milliken and Martins 1996).

Some other benefits of diverse work groups include attracting and retaining superior performers, higher levels of innovation, stimulation of creativity, lower operating costs, more creative problem solving, and increased organizational flexibility (Ng and Tung 1998). Diverse work groups can also help to reduce the various forms of "isms," such as ablebodiedism, ageism, classism, ethnocentrism, heterosexism, racism, and sexism. In all phases of recruitment, hiring, and retention processes, managers should strive to increase diversity in the workplace.

A logical first step in creating and nurturing a diverse workplace is to perform an objective assessment of where the organization is in terms of policies and procedures, and to measure staff attitudes and perceptions with regard to the library's commitment to promoting diversity. The Association of College and Research Libraries (ACRL) (2012) has created ClimateQUAL® (https://www.climatequal.org/home) for just this purpose. ClimateQUAL® is an online survey that examines the organizational climate in terms of staff beliefs and attitudes, current supervisory practices, fairness, learning, diversity, and teamwork. Results from ClimateQUAL® can be used to guide diversity training and initiatives.

Here are some practical ways to promote workplace diversity, especially during the recruitment phase (adapted from the *Wall Street Journal*'s "How-To Guide on Increasing Workplace Diversity"):

1. Develop a strategy that supports hiring a workforce that resembles the community you serve.
2. Ask current staff members to provide referrals (this supports the added benefit that they may be able to assist the new employee with their transition).
3. Contact other community organizations for help with finding candidates.
   a. Cultural and nonprofit institutions
   b. Local colleges
   c. Churches
4. Provide and support diversity training opportunities across the organization.
   a. Make the recruiting process transparent.
   b. Make sure managers know, understand, and can communicate the benefits of a diverse workplace.
5. If you do not already have one, develop an equal opportunity employment policy.
   a. Include meritorious hiring practices.
   b. Ensure hiring practices are neutral with regard to age, race, gender, and minority.
   c. Create a committee to help implement policy if needed.
      i. Suggest new ideas on attracting more diverse staff.
      ii. Ensure mission statement reflects any changes.
6. Give new hires reasons to stay.
   a. Within the organization
      i. Expand benefits:
         1. Childcare subsidies, flexible schedules
         2. Accommodate cultural and religious holidays.
      ii. Familiarize new hires with the organizational culture.
         1. Provide mentors.
         2. Foster relationships with other staff.
         3. Provide opportunities for interaction across departments.
   b. Within the community
      i. Work with local business organizations and chamber of commerce.
      ii. Promote cultural offerings, ethnic restaurants, markets, international movies.

The American Library Association Office for Diversity, Literacy and Outreach Services (ODLOS; www.ala.org/offices/diversity) and its member groups offer an extensive variety of free resources for libraries that pertain to promoting diversity. These range from issue briefs and resource lists to outreach tool kits and samples of diversity plans. They also provide well-spelled-out strategies for recruitment practices and guidelines for how to create standards that ensure a diverse workplace.

The ACRL also provides a set of eleven standards for diversity based on the National Association of Social Workers (2015) *Standards for Cultural Competence in Social Work Practice*. Though they are primarily aimed at academic libraries and institutes of higher education, library directors and managers in any setting will likely gain insight and guidance from review of the standards. Individuals in management positions, and those who have supervisory duties, should also familiarize themselves, staff members, and their administrative oversight personnel with the guidelines as well, especially if there are not existing diversity action plans and initiatives already in place.

Cultural competency is a key component of an inclusive organization (ACRL 2012). Cultural competency has been succinctly defined as the "ability to interact effectively with those from different backgrounds and cultures" (Adams, Bell, and Griffin 2007). To instill inclusive ideals, incorporate cultural competency as a staff skills requirement and offer regular training opportunities and workshops on diversity issues.

Cultural competency of course begins on an individual level but is a characteristic of organizations too. Included here are the ACRL's guidelines for the culturally competent organization, which should be considered for adoption by all libraries:

- Develop an action plan to actively recruit and retain staff and librarians. Librarians should go beyond the traditional avenues to advertise positions to create and develop formal and informal ways to reach individuals that represent the constituents served.
- Obtain statistics about underrepresented personnel (students, staff, librarians) in the organization review information, and work to understand the lacking numbers and personnel in the organization.
- Develop and implement human resource and other organizational policies, procedures, and practices that support staff diversity.
- Develop and implement organizational policies, procedures, and practices that effectively address the dynamics of a diverse workforce.
- Review recruitment, hiring, and promotion policies, procedures, and practices to remedy inadvertent exclusion of or discrimination toward underrepresented, underserved, and historically oppressed groups.

- Implement safeguards against exclusion of or discrimination toward under-represented, underserved, and historically oppressed groups in the workplace, and take corrective action when inequities are discovered.

Once you have worked to increase diversity and are successful in hiring new staff, endeavor to ensure they have continued support. As they may not be well connected in the new community, offer aid in their adjustment process. Make them feel welcomed and communicate their value to other members in the organization. If things do not work out for any reason and they do decide to leave, be sure to have an exit interview process to learn what might have been done differently. Be willing to respond to suggestions for improvement and to learn from mistakes. Additionally, as with all new hires, consider the use of a probationary period, so that both staff and administration are not permanently locked into an untenable or undesirable spot.

Beyond diversity in hiring, attention should also be paid to providing services to diverse populations. According to the International Federation of Library Association (IFLA) Library Services to Multicultural Populations Section, successful delivery of services to culturally diverse communities is dependent upon the library staff. The necessary qualities and skills include the ability to communicate positively, to understand users' needs, to cooperate with individuals and groups, and to have a knowledge and understanding of cultural diversity (IFLA 2011). They have created a useful tool kit outlining templates and strategies for understanding and promoting multicultural services that are appropriate for library communities (IFLA Toolkit).

In addition to diversity in service provision, attention should also be paid to promoting diversity through library materials and resources. While treatment of this subject is beyond the scope of this volume, it is worth pointing out the grassroots movement under way to promote more diversity in children's publishing: We Need Diverse Books (weneeddiversebooks.org). Their mission is "putting more books featuring diverse characters into the hands of all children," and their inclusionary vision is "a world in which all children can see themselves in the pages of a book" (We Need Diverse Books 2016).

IN CLOSING

Some years ago, I attended a management seminar on dealing with "problem employees." The presenter started out by making the point that all of the attendees were likely perfectionists and that our key takeaway from the workshop was that we should "lower our expectations of staff," and that if we did, our jobs would be easier and we would be much happier overall. Now that I have had time to reflect on this advice, I have to admit I respectfully disagree. An alternative approach, to endeavor to nurture staff and their individual and collective development, is likely to engender better results all the way 'round. Given the wide and varied range of personalities, backgrounds, and training of individuals in any workplace, and the changes in service provision and specific work tasks that might need to be performed, this may not always be as easy or straightforward as we would like.

A good place to start is with an ardent commitment and ongoing dedication to developing staff, with careful attention to their long-term professional and personal growth. After all, it is the employees who are responsible for making the work happen so that the organization remains healthy and thrives. When staff are valued and nurtured, the workplace is not only more pleasant and productive, but it becomes easier to attract and retain high-level employees. In this way, a positive cycle can be created and maintained. Because staff are truly the most important resource in any library organization, creating an environment where there is sincere interest in and dedication to their well-being is the best investment a supervisor or manager can make.

This can be achieved by setting a positive and supportive tone, valuing open communication, exerting influence as necessary, identifying and cultivating staff members' unique gifts, providing consistency, keeping up-to-date with changes in the field, and leading by example. If libraries are to continue to fulfill their profound institutional and societal roles and to remain relevant during times of rapid change, it is imperative that all staff are given the continuous and sustentative support they require to thrive and to shine.

BIBLIOGRAPHY

Adams, Maurianne, Lee Anne Bell, and Pat Griffin (eds.). 2007. *Teaching for Diversity and Social Justice*, 2nd edition. New York: Routledge.

Association of College and Research Libraries. Diversity Standards: Cultural Competency for Academic Libraries, 2012, accessed January 31, 2017, http://www.ala.org/acrl/standards/diversity.

Bernard, Tristan. 1921. In Bartlett, John, *Familiar Quotations*, 16th edition, Justin Kaplan, ed., 600. Boston, MA: Little Brown & Company, 1992.

Coehlo, Paolo. 1993. *The Alchemist*. New York: HarperTorch, p. 150.

"How to Increase Workplace Diversity." *Wall Street Journal*, accessed January 31, 2017, http://guides.wsj.com/management/building-a-workplace-culture/how-to-increase-workplace-diversity/.

International Federation of Library Associations and Institutions. Section on Library Services to Multicultural Populations. July 2011. *Multicultural Communities: Guidelines for Library Services: An Overview*, accessed January 3, 2017, http://

www.ifla.org/files/assets/library-services-to-multicultural-populations/publications/guidelines-overview-en.pdf.

Joyce, Kevin E. 2003. "Lessons for Employers from Fortune's '100 best.'" *Business Horizons* 46 (2): 77–84.

Madlock, Paul E. 2008. "The Link between Leadership Style, Communicator Competence, and Employee Satisfaction." *Journal of Business Communication* 45 (1): 61–78.

Milliken, Frances and Luis Martins. April 1996. "Searching for Common Threads: Understanding the Multiple Effects of Diversity in Organizational Groups." *Academy of Management Review* 21 (2): 402–433.

Ng, Eddy, and Rosalie Tung. December 1998. "Ethno-Cultural Diversity and Organizational Effectiveness: A Field Study." *International Journal of Human Resource Management* 9 (6): 980–995.

"Our Mission." We Need Diverse Books, accessed January 31, 2017, http://weneeddiversebooks.org/mission-statement/.

Pfeffer, Jeffrey, and John F. Veiga. 1999. "Putting People First for Organizational Success." *The Academy of Management Executive* 13 (2): 37–48.

"Standards and Indicators for Cultural Competence in Social Work Practice." Practice and Professional Development. National Association of Social Workers, 2015, accessed May 7, 2017, https://www.socialworkers.org/practice/standards/Standards _and_Indicators_for_Cultural_Competence.asp.

Index

advertisements. *See* job advertisements
ALA. *See* American Library Association
American Library Association (ALA),
 9, 79, 84–89, 119–121, 132
appeals, 61–68, 109–111

certification, 18, 84, 85
communication, 5, 53, 75, 103, 126–128
conferences, 31, 84, 107
continuing education, 79–83, 109, 116,
 120
cross-training, 24–25, 82

degree programs, 85
descriptions. *See* job descriptions
diversity, 39, 119, 130–133

empowerment, 9, 93
engagement, 46–52
evaluation, 39, 40, 75, 93–95

feedback, 94–97, 106–108
fellowships, 117–120
flexibility, 51–53, 132
foundations, 120, 122–123
fun, 54–55, 130
funding, 22, 109, 115–124

goals, 48, 50, 56, 93–98, 100
grants, 115–124

hiring, 11, 21, 29, 30, 40–42, 131–133

interviews, 36–38, 69

job advertisements, 32–34
job descriptions, 18, 21, 107
job sharing, 52–53
job splitting, 53–54

mentoring, 87–89
Medical Library Association (MLA),
 31, 75, 83, 85, 87, 120, 121
MLA. *See* Medical Library
 Association
motivation, 45–49, 82, 93

online resources, 32, 83

paraprofessionals, 16–17, 85
peer review, 61, 94, 95
performance appraisal, 99–112
plans, 10–15, 128
policies, 5–6, 109, 132
procedures, 5–6, 96, 132

professional associations. *See* professional organizations
professional organizations, 31, 84, 87, 119–121
progressive discipline, 56–60

recruitment, 29–31, 54, 131, 132
rubric, 38–40

samples: continuing education policy, 80–82; job description, 18–20; performance review appeal form, 109–111; performance review form, 100–106; survey, 76–77; written warning, 59–60
surveys, 50, 75, 77–79, 130
sustainability, 124

team building, 51, 106, 129–130
tenure, 21–23

workshops, 84

About the Author

Mary Grace Flaherty is an assistant professor in the School of Information and Library Science at the University of North Carolina at Chapel Hill. She received her PhD from Syracuse University and holds master's degrees from Johns Hopkins University and the University of Maryland. Over the course of her career, she has worked in a variety of library settings, including academic, health research, public, and special. Her teaching responsibilities include courses in health sciences information, management issues in libraries, collection development, disaster planning, proposal development, and public libraries.